MW01123100

CURRENT ISSUES IN AMERICAN POLITICS

CURRENT ISSUES IN AMERICAN POLITICS: A NEW YORK TIMES READER

Gregory M. Scott, Editor
University of Central Oklahoma

PRENTICE HALL, UPPER SADDLE RIVER, NEW JERSEY 07458

Library of Congress Cataloging-in-Publication Data

Current issues in American politics: a New York Times reader/
    Gregory M. Scott, editor.
        p.   cm.
    Includes bibliographical references.
    ISBN 0-13-977505-6
    1. Political planning—United States.   2. United States—Politics
and government—1993–   I. Scott, Gregory M.
JK468.P64C87   1999
    320.973—dc21   99-37190
                                                                  CIP

Editorial director: Charlyce Jones Owen
Editor in chief: Nancy Roberts
Senior acquisitions editor: Beth Gillett Mejia
Editorial assistant: Brian Prybella
Marketing manager: Christopher DeJohn
Editorial/production supervision: Kari Callaghan Mazzola
Electronic page makeup: Kari Callaghan Mazzola
Interior design: John P. Mazzola
Cover director: Jayne Conte
Cover design: Bruce Kenselaar
Buyer: Ben Smith

This book was set in 10/12 Meridien by Big Sky Composition
and was printed and bound by Courier Companies, Inc.
The cover was printed by Phoenix Color Corp.

© 2000 by Prentice-Hall, Inc.
Upper Saddle River, New Jersey 07458

Printed in the United States of America
10   9   8   7   6   5   4   3   2   1

ISBN 0-13-977505-6

PRENTICE-HALL INTERNATIONAL (UK) LIMITED, *London*
PRENTICE-HALL OF AUSTRALIA PTY. LIMITED, *Sydney*
PRENTICE-HALL CANADA INC., *Toronto*
PRENTICE-HALL HISPANOAMERICANA, S.A., *Mexico*
PRENTICE-HALL OF INDIA PRIVATE LIMITED, *New Delhi*
PRENTICE-HALL OF JAPAN, INC., *Tokyo*
PEARSON EDUCATION ASIA PTE. LTD., *Singapore*
EDITORA PRENTICE-HALL DO BRASIL, LTDA., *Rio de Janeiro*

CONTENTS

PREFACE

As political scientists have long known, the *New York Times* (*NYT*) is one of the most thorough and reliable sources of news in the world today. *Current Issues in American Politics: A New York Times Reader* provides students with the opportunity to learn about five of the great political debates of the turn of the millennium while becoming familiar with the high quality articles the *NYT* offers. In addition, an introduction, debate questions, and suggested sources of more information (including leading internet sites and recent books) are provided for each of the five issues.

The issues selected for this book are perennial. Although they emerge and recede from the political scene from one month to the next, they reveal fundamental differences in public opinion:

- Tobacco, used in this country by Native Americans since at least 1100, became controversial as soon as it was introduced in Europe by early traders and explorers, and is today blamed for more deaths than any other single cause.
- Gun control, as the materials in this book illustrate, is about more than sportsmanship. It concerns our deepest fears and needs for security.
- While the immigration debate was not salient in the 1996 presidential election, it is a constant concern in California, New York, and Texas, and is beginning to reemerge as a vital concern for the first half of the twenty-first century.
- When Alabama's Governor Fob James ran for reelection in 1998, he stridently supported school prayer, believing his Bible Belt constituency would affirm his beliefs, but he was sorely mistaken. His

defeat drew the attention of Religious Right activists across the country to the potential unpopularity of the school prayer cause. This election, however, has by no means decided the issue.

■ The bilingual education movement has run headlong into opponents who support "English only" laws. While the English-only forces won a major battle in California this year, bilingual education advocates promise a comeback.

While an attempt has been made to represent arguments for both sides of each issue, a balanced, objective analysis is not the primary goal of this text. Rather, the goal of this text is to present issues in a manner that catches the reader's imagination and inspires him or her to join the ongoing discussions that shape our nation's future.

Gregory M. Scott

CURRENT ISSUES IN AMERICAN POLITICS

1

THE TOBACCO WARS

Today, nearly 3,000 young people across our country will begin smoking regularly. Of these 3,000 young people, 1,000 will lose that gamble to the diseases caused by smoking. The net effect of this is that among children living in America today, 5 million will die an early preventable death because of a decision made as a child.

—Donna E. Shalala, Ph.D., Secretary of Health and Human Services,
Testimony before the Senate Labor and Human
Resources Committee, September 25, 1997

On October 12, 1492, Christopher Columbus set a Spanish banner in the sand of a land he named, in dedication to the founder of Christianity, San Salvador. Stowing the fruit and spears offered by the Arawak "Indians" who so politely greeted him, the imperious Italian explorer tossed away the strange brown tobacco leaves his generous if naive native hosts seemed to treasure. Columbus's rude and ignorant disposal might be called the first round in the "tobacco wars," the long-standing fatal animosity between the broad-leafed plant's detractors and defenders.

If Mildred Wiley's coworkers had followed Columbus's example, tossing their weed in the can, the 56-year-old Marion, Indiana, resident might still be alive today. Instead, in 1991 Mildred became a secondary-smoke-induced lung cancer statistic: one of the more than four hundred thousand people who died in the United States that year of causes directly linked to smoking. The impact of smoking is astounding. Forty-seven million Americans now smoke. Although about 400,000 Americans died in World

War II, our nation's most fatal war, more than that number—430,000—of our relatives, friends, and neighbors die from smoking every year.

If cigarette smoking is the nation's leading cause of death, why does the tobacco industry have so many influential supporters? Why, for example, has Howard Baker, former Tennessee senator and hero of the Senate Watergate committee, become a lobbyist for tobacco companies? Money. In the past decade they have hired, in addition to Baker, several other highly influential lobbyists, and for their efforts have gained support from representatives in states that do not produce significant tobacco crops, such as Oklahoma's Senator Don Nickles.

Tobacco enthusiasts point to a long history of support for enjoyment of a variety of tobacco products. Native Americans have smoked for recreational and religious purposes since at least 1100 c.e. Jean Nicot de Villemain, French ambassador to Portugal, commended the herb to the sixteenth century French court and his name later became attached to the world's most highly addictive chemical, nicotine. Just like thousands of elementary school students today, in 1601 Sir Walter Raleigh became a smoking enabler by lighting up his friend, England's Queen Elizabeth.

Although Jamestown's John Rolfe grew the New World's first commercial tobacco crop in 1614, widespread production, manufacture, and sale of tobacco developed in the mid-eighteenth century. Southern planters including George Washington planted substantial crops before the Revolution. In 1761 Pierre Lorillard began manufacturing snuff, cigars, and pipe tobacco in New York City. In 1847 Philip Morris opened a store in London to sell Turkish cigarettes, and two years later J. E. Liggett opened a shop in St. Louis. By 1860, 348 Virginia factories produced chewing tobacco and Bull Durham cigarettes became popular. By 1920, per capita cigarette consumption exceeded 400 per year.

Tobacco's opponents also boast a long and colorful heritage, however. In the eyes of our society's antismoking forces, cigarette companies are more dangerous than the German machine guns that ripped hundreds of American troops to shreds on Normandy's bloody beaches, and smoking opponents have sometimes employed violence in their cause. Pope Urban VIII (1623–44) wanted to excommunicate people who defiled his cathedrals with snuff or smoke. In 1633 Turkey's Sultan Murad IV executed up to eighteen "infidels" a day for the sin and crime of smoking, and the following year Russia's Tsar Alexis ordered, for the first smoking offense, whipping, nose slitting, and deportation to Siberia, and execution for the second offense. In 1939 Adolf Hitler's lieutenant Hermann Goering restricted his troops' smoking while conducting their official duties. Goering seemed to understand that it is difficult to subdue the world and eliminate "undesirable" people while fighting off emphysema.

American antitobacco forces have waged their war primarily through exercise of the democratic process. Regulation and taxation of tobacco predates this nation's founding. In 1758 the colonial Virginian Assembly passed the Two Penny Act, instantly unpopular because it forbade paying government salaries in percentages of the tobacco crop. Congress levied its first tax on tobacco in 1794. Contemporary liability suits against the manufacturers began in 1963 when Philip Morris won its first round in court. But in 1997 Liggett Myers settled with twenty-two states, and was forced to admit that smoking is hazardous to health, something that came as no revelation at all to health researchers. As early as 1761, English physicians John Hill and Percival Pott noted high correlations between snuff and nose cancer, and between soot encountered by chimney sweeps and scrotum cancer. In a long series of announcements beginning in 1964, the U.S. surgeon general has divulged results of studies linking smoking to heart disease, cancer, and numerous other ailments.

In the 1997 settlement Liggett also had to admit that tobacco advertising had successfully targeted youth. In 1921, for example, R. J. Reynolds introduced its "I'd Walk a Mile for a Camel" campaign, and seven decades later preschoolers could identify Joe Camel as easily as Mickey Mouse.

Both sides in the tobacco wars claim victories. In 1987 smoking was prohibited in domestic airline flights of two hours or less duration, a ban that has been extended to all flights today. California, New York, and other states have excluded smoking from restaurants and other public buildings. Since 1973 cigarette advertising has been banned from television and confined to magazines and billboards.

Tobacco companies, however, have probably won the greater battles. In what at first looked like a defeat, cigarette manufacturers placed surgeon general's warnings on cigarette packs. Antitobacco forces soon discovered, however, that the warnings did little to inhibit smoking, and in fact shielded tobacco companies from suits. Tobacco lawyers successfully argued for two decades that since people were warned of the adverse affects of smoking, the manufacturers were therefore absolved of liability (i.e., people who are duly warned smoke at their own risk). Even the recent settlements described in the *New York Times* articles in this volume have not seriously harmed the tobacco companies. Their stock remains strong because they simply pass the costs of settling the suits on to consumers in the form of price increases. What is the real issue with respect to tobacco? As you read the following *New York Times* articles (on pages 5–16), make a list of what you perceive to be the real issues in the continuing tobacco debate.

The New York Times

November 24, 1998

Cigarette Makers Announce
Large Price Rise

By Barry Meier

Smokers will soon feel the effect of the new $206 billion tobacco settlement deal, as leading cigarette makers said yesterday that they would raise wholesale prices by the largest amount in history.

Both the Philip Morris Companies Inc., the producer of Marlboro brand cigarettes, and R. J. Reynolds Tobacco Company, a unit of RJR Nabisco Holdings Corporation, the producer of Winston brand cigarettes, said they would raise cigarette prices 45 cents a package. Analysts had predicted that producers might raise wholesale prices sharply yesterday as the industry signed a huge legal settlement with 46 states over litigation brought against tobacco companies to recover health care costs related to smoking.

But the price increases were somewhat higher than expected, and the two other major companies that participated in the tobacco accord, Brown & Williamson Tobacco—owned by B.A.T. Industries P.L.C.—and Lorillard Tobacco—owned by Loews Corporation—are expected to follow suit.

"This is the biggest price increase in dollar terms in the history of the United States," David Adelman, an analyst with Morgan Stanley Dean Witter, told The Associated Press.

The price increase, if passed along fully to consumers, would raise the average cost of a package of cigarettes to $2.45.

But in the cigarette industry, the full effect of such price increases is not always felt by the consumer because competitive discounting by manufacturers takes place on the wholesale level.

Following settlements over the past year with four states—Florida, Minnesota, Mississippi and Texas—under which the tobacco industry agreed to pay a total of $40 billion over 25 years, producers announced wholesale price increases of 20 cents a pack to reflect the cost of those settlements. But for competitive reasons, some makers did not pass those price increases through on all their brands, in order to gain marketplace advantages over their rivals.

Still, Mr. Adelman said, smokers might see a price increase this time of about 50 cents a pack, if distributors and retailers add a nickel to the wholesale price increase. The national average price of a pack of cigarettes is $1.95.

Analysts have put the cost of the settlement plan with the 46 states at about 35 to 40 cents a pack. Under the accord, the $206 billion would be paid over 25 years.

But industry officials made no secret in settlement talks that the cost of the accord would be borne by smokers.

The prospect of such a price increase was the thrust of a furious attack by the tobacco industry on a $516 billion tobacco bill defeated in the Senate this year. That bill would have raised the price of a pack of cigarettes by $1.10, and the industry began a $50 million advertising campaign depicting it as a tax-and-spend bill that would only take money out of the pockets of smokers.

That campaign was credited in part for the bill's defeat.

Some analysts had believed that the companies would introduce price increase[s] reflecting the cost of the latest settlement plan slowly. But last Friday, after 46 state officials signed on to the agreement, Gary Black, a tobacco industry analyst with Sanford C. Bernstein, an investment company, said he believed that producers would announce massive price increases yesterday.

Under the settlement plan, manufacturers agreed to make a number of marketing changes, including removing all tobacco billboards and no longer giving away or selling merchandise like caps emblazoned with the brand names of cigarettes.

As a result of the agreements on marketing changes, Federal regulators said yesterday they planned to drop their case against R. J. Reynolds, which they had accused of harming children with its Joe Camel advertising campaign.

Lawyers for the Federal Trade Commission said they would file a motion to dismiss the case because the tobacco deal would achieve the objectives of banning cartoon characters in tobacco advertising and financing anti-tobacco campaigns directed toward youths.

"We believe that continuing this litigation in light of the state settlement would serve no public purpose and would be merely a waste of resources," a trade commission lawyer, Joel Winston, told an administrative law judge at a hearing.

The settlement brings to an end state lawsuits filed to recover Medicaid funds spent treating smoking related diseases. Along with the 46 states it covers, the newest accord applies to five United States territories.

The New York Times

November 29, 1998

Tobacco Profits May Soar,
FTC Study Shows

By John M. Broder

WASHINGTON—Tobacco industry profits could soar under terms of a legal settlement proposed in June by 40 state attorneys general and cigarette makers, according to a new analysis of the agreement by the Federal Trade Commission.

The study found that the tobacco companies could reap as much as $123 billion in additional profits in the next 25 years if the settlement plan was adopted as drafted.

The analysis, conducted in response to a request from Congress, also concluded that the $368.5 billion face value of the settlement was significantly overstated. The real cost to industry is about $207 billion because the companies' payments are to fall as cigarette consumption drops, the commission staff report found. The cost to industry of the June agreement is about $100 billion in today's dollars, the study found.

The settlement proposal is unlikely to be enacted by Congress without substantial changes, if at all. But the trade commission's findings are startling because the agreement has been depicted as extremely costly to the cigarette industry. Instead, the agency found, the industry would thrive financially while enjoying immunity from most litigation.

Scott Williams, a spokesman for the tobacco makers, said that the report was "highly speculative and misses the point." Williams, of the public relations firm Bozell Swayer Miller Group, said that the purpose of the settlement proposal was to reduce smoking by minors, not to maximize industry profits.

He declined to comment on the specific findings of the study.

The report said that the industry's potential windfall profits would result from the cigarette companies' raising prices much more than was necessary to cover the cost of the settlement. The tobacco industry historically has increased prices more quickly than its costs have risen, taking advantage of the small number of companies in the cigarette market and the millions of customers addicted to its products.

But the trade commission study may already be largely obsolete, because President Clinton has rejected many parts of the June proposal, including the provision allowing the companies to pass along to smokers all of the costs of the settlement.

Under the president's proposal, cigarette prices would rise by as much as $1.50 a pack, but a substantial portion of the increase would be captured by the government in the form of penalties if smoking by teen-agers did not drop sharply.

The study also assumes that the cigarette companies will enjoy a $50 billion tax break passed as part of the July balanced-budget accord. But both houses of Congress voted overwhelmingly in the past two weeks to rescind the tax break.

Trade commission officials said that repeal of the tax break would reduce long-term industry profits by an unspecified amount.

Robert Pitofsky, the trade commission chairman, said that the June accord contained an "extremely unusual" anti-trust exemption that would allow the cigarette makers to "jointly confer, coordinate or act in concert" to achieve the goals of the settlement.

He said that the exemption would permit the tobacco companies to collude to impose price increases far in excess of those required to cover the annual payments of roughly $15 billion required by the proposal.

"Taken at its worst, this exemption would allow the companies to get in a room and decide among themselves what is the best level of prices and what is the appropriate level of profits," Pitofsky said.

He noted that such collusive activity was ordinarily a violation of criminal anti-trust statutes.

Rep. Marty Meehan, D-Mass., welcomed Pitofsky's conclusion that the anti-trust exemption was too broad.

"We now know that the exemption provides the industry with benefits that go far beyond the original justification," said Meehan, co-chairman of the congressional task force on tobacco, which requested the report. "It allows them to increase profits into the next millennium and puts them in a better economic position than they are now."

Separately, a CBS News poll showed that a large majority of the public doubted that the proposed agreement would significantly reduce the number of teen-agers who smoked.

Only 19 percent of a national sample of 1,051 adults surveyed late last week said they believed the accord would reduce the number of teen-agers who begin smoking. Some 75 percent said it would not.

By a 2 to 1 margin, the respondents—half of whom are current or former smokers—said that the Government and the tobacco industry could not take steps that would significantly reduce tobacco use by minors.

The New York Times

Sunday, November 29, 1998

Smokescreen: The Ifs and Buts of the Tobacco Settlement

By Sylvia Nasar

Last week's $206 billion settlement between the tobacco industry and 46 states is supposed to put Big Tobacco on the run. The agreement requires cigarette makers to compensate states for the medical costs of treating smoking-related diseases. It's been hailed as a triumph of the public interest over special interests. But a closer look at the hard economics behind the agreement reveals something quite different.

The problem, economists and legal experts who have studied the deal say, isn't that the damages won by the states are too small, as leaders of the anti-smoking lobby complain. It's that 99 percent of the total settlement is really a disguised tax hike.

Taxing cigarettes more heavily may or may not be a good idea, the critics say, but labeling as "damages" what is effectively a sales tax is misleading and will create a boondoggle for trial lawyers and a windfall for the smaller tobacco companies.

Under the deal, the Big Four tobacco producers will wind up paying direct damages of at most 1 percent of the settlement total, or $2.4 billion. That amount, calculated as a proportion of the companies' current market value, is to be paid regardless of how many packs of cigarettes they sell in the future.

The rest of the $206 billion will be paid by smokers: Cigarette prices are expected to climb by an average of about 35 cents a pack.

"Reasonable people can disagree whether increasing the cigarette tax is a good or bad idea," said Jeremy Bulow, the incoming chief economist of the Federal Trade Commission. "But the reason that the attorneys general don't want to call it a tax is so they can claim a political victory."

Clearly investors thought the deal was worth celebrating.

On Nov. 20, the day the attorneys general announced the settlement, the stock of the leading tobacco companies soared. Investors chose to disbelieve that an industry with profits of $5 billion a year would be paying $8 billion a year in damages for the next 25 years. Instead, the investors gave credence to stock analysts who believe that the profits of tobacco companies will decline by a maximum of 10 percent. And cigarette producers wasted no time in raising prices—a day after the settlement was signed on Monday, two major companies raised prices 45 cents a pack.

The higher prices represent what is essentially an old-fashioned sales tax, the very kind of tax that the Republican Congress shot down a few months back as "big government."

What makes it a tax? The fact that the amount paid is to rise and fall with the number of cigarette packs sold.

Like many sales taxes, it is borne primarily by the consumer. "Every single cigarette tax ever passed has been paid fully by the consumer," said John Gruber, an economist at the Massachusetts Institute of Technology and a former deputy treasury secretary. "There's no reason to think this will be any different."

"If it looks like a duck, quacks like a duck ...," Mr. Gruber added. "It's a tax because it's a set of payments made by tobacco companies that depend on how many packs they sell."

Still, most economists think it makes sense to use taxes to have the price of cigarettes reflect their true social cost, though some, like Mr. Bulow, have reservations because the taxes fall heavily on the poor. And as tobacco companies have known for years, the evidence is compelling that raising prices leads some smokers to cut back and deters teen-agers from picking up the habit.

But by disguising a de facto sales tax as damages, the critics maintain, the states have agreed to a deal with unintended consequences that are just hinted at in the joint news release describing the 100-page settlement. By calling taxes damages, the critics say, the states wound up agreeing to provisions that Congress would never dream of if it passed a tax increase.

For example, economists cite the huge contingency fees that the 200 or so trial lawyers who helped produce the agreement will collect. Under the deal, the lawyers will divide $1.25 billion initially and about $500 million a year thereafter. That's an $8 billion payout, or 20 times the biggest contingency fee ever paid, the $400 million collected by a lawyer in the 1985 Texaco-Pennzoil case.

Mr. Gruber calls the legal fees "huge, gross and disgusting." Mr. Bulow estimates that had the fees been calculated only on the basis of actual damages, each lawyer would receive an average of about $1 million apiece, versus the $40 million apiece that the lawyers will actually collect.

"By calling the settlement 'damages' it makes it seem reasonable to pay the lawyers a lot," said Paul Klemperer, an economist at Oxford University. "If you called it taxes, you wouldn't expect to give lawyers a fraction of the tax."

The lawyers maintain they are being paid fairly for taking a huge gamble. But for one thing, some states hadn't even got around to filing suits against the tobacco companies, so the lawyers in those states haven't done much of anything yet. And those lawyers who have put in time did most of their work in the past year—after it became clear that a broad settlement was a near-certain bet.

A second consequence of calling taxes damages is that the deal, far from inflicting pain on all cigarette producers, actually enriches a few of them. Take Liggett & Myers, which until recently was valued at about $120 million and which hadn't turned a profit in several years. Under the deal, Liggett will actually collect an annual subsidy of about $100 million, courtesy of taxpayers.

Here's how. A tax hike applies to all cigarette producers, big and small, current and future. But the states can only collect damages from the companies they are suing: in this case, the Big Four: Philip Morris, R. J. Reynolds Tobacco, Lorillard Tobacco and Brown & Williamson Tobacco.

But by limiting damages to the largest companies, the states would be handing smaller tobacco producers like Liggett a cost advantage of 35 cents a pack, since the Big Four would have to raise their prices, while the little guys would not. Given that it costs just 20 cents to manufacture a pack of cigarettes, that's a huge advantage.

How did the states solve the problem? In effect, they told the small companies that if they agreed to be "taxed" they would be allowed—up to a limit higher than their current sales—to keep the revenue they collected instead of turning them in to the states. Thus, Liggett can match the higher prices charged by the Big Four companies but doesn't have to hand over any of the extra income except in the unlikely event that its sales exceed 400 million packs, or 125 percent of its current sales.

Even assuming that Liggett loses some sales when it raises its prices, Mr. Klemperer said, the subsidy it will collect still amounts to $100 million a year, an amount equal to its recent market value.

Actually, Liggett gained even more from the tobacco agreement. Because of agreements reached earlier with some states, Liggett wasn't as vulnerable as the other companies to states' threats to pass punitive legislation if it failed to climb aboard. To induce Liggett to sign on, Philip Morris, eager to dispel the threat of a firm that could potentially produce cigarettes at a 35-cent cost advantage, paid three times the value of the entire company for 3 of Liggett's 14 brands. The contract stipulated that Philip Morris would pay Liggett $150 million even if the Federal Trade Commission shoots down the deal.

Ian Ayres, a professor at the Yale Law School, is among those worried about the precedent set by the settlement. "It's scary," he said.

QUESTIONS FOR CLASS DISCUSSION OR DEBATE

As you read the *New York Times* articles and conduct further research, many questions may come to your mind. If you plan to debate tobacco issues in class, you may want to consider arguing positions related to the following statements:

- The right to smoke is guaranteed by the Constitution of the United States.
- Tobacco companies should be held responsible for illness and death caused by smoking.
- Raising the cigarette tax merely increases taxes and promotes big government.
- Smoking is essentially an economic, rather than a moral or political issue.
- A cigarette tax is a disadvantage to poor people.

RESOURCES FOR CLASS DEBATES AND FURTHER STUDY

THE TOBACCO WARS ON THE INTERNET

In the address box on your web browser, type the following address: www12.nytimes.com/library/politics/tobacco-weblinks.html. Here you will find an updated list, prepared by the *New York Times*, of web sites related to the tobacco controversy. An illustration of the types of materials that may be found on that page appears below.

The *New York Times* Tobacco Debate on the Web

Documents

Tobacco documents released by the House Commerce Committee
Attorneys General Liggett Settlement Agreement March 20, 1997
State Tobacco Information Center
The State of Minnesota and Blue Cross/Blue Shield of Minnesota vs. Philip Morris Inc.
Blue Cross and Blue Shield of Minnesota
Tobacco Home Page

Tobacco Debate

Court TV Tobacco Litigation Library
Action on Smoking and Health
American Cancer Society

American Smokers Alliance
National Smokers Alliance
Smoke-Free Kids and Soccer
Tobacco BBS
Food and Drug Administration, Home Page
Food and Drug Administration, Children, and Tobacco

Tobacco Business

The Tobacco Resolution, a Web site from the Tobacco Companies
    perspective
R. J. Reynolds Tobacco Company home page
Brown and Williamson Tobacco Corp.
United Stated Department of Agriculture
USDA/AMS—Tobacco Division Home Page
Alcohol Tobacco and Firearms, Tobacco Programs
National Farmers Union
http://www.house.gov/commerce/TobaccoDocs/documents.html

FURTHER REFERENCE

Caulfield Rybak, Deborah, and David Phelps. *Smoked: The Inside Story of the Minnesota Tobacco Trial.* MSP Books. 1998.
Gall, Timothy L., and Daniel M. Lucas, eds. *Statistics on Alcohol, Drug and Tobacco Use: A Selection of Statistical Charts, Graphs and Tables About Alcohol, Drug and Tobacco Use from a Variety of Sources.* Gale Research. 1995.
Grossman, David. *Tobacco Smoking and the Law.* Lexis Law Publications. 1992.
Jacobson, Peter D., and Jeffrey Wasserman. *Tobacco Control Laws: Implementation and Enforcement.* Rand Corporation. 1997.
Kluger, Richard. *Ashes to Ashes: America's Hundred-Year Cigarette War, the Public Health, and the Unabashed Triumph of Philip Morris.* Vintage Books. 1997.
Leitner, David L., ed. *Tobacco-Related Litigation and Insurance.* American Bar Association. 1997.
Mollenkamp, Carrick, Adam Levy, Joseph Menn, and Jeffrey Rothfeder. *The People vs. Big Tobacco: How the States Took On the Cigarette Giants.* Bloomberg Press. 1998.
Nijhoff, Martinus. *Legislative Responses to Tobacco Use.* 1991.
Pringle, Peter. *Cornered: Big Tobacco at the Bar of Justice.* Henry Holt & Company, Inc. 1998.

2

GUN CONTROL

The Greek word for fear is φοβοσ (fobos). Using this word as a suffix, psychologists have named many fears, or phobias. *Arachnophobia* is fear of spiders. *Claustrophobia* is fear of enclosed spaces. *Agoraphobia* is fear of open spaces. *Logophobia* is fear of words. *Gephyrophobia* is fear of crossing bridges. *Kakorrhaphiophobia* is fear of failure. *Triskaidekaphobia* is fear of the number thirteen.

What does fear have to do with gun control? Consider the first article in this section (on pages 23–24), regarding the Columbine High School incident, which provides yet another example of people with guns killing other people (and themselves). Incidents like the one at Columbine High School often exacerbate people's fears and spur renewed attempts at gun control (as well as the subsequent reactions to those attempts).

The gun control issue actually arises from a number of different fears, but people on both sides of the gun control debate do suffer from two common fears: Most people, having committed private indiscretions, secretly fear the potentially destructive forces within themselves; and likewise, they fear the potentially destructive forces within others. Both gun control advocates and gun control opponents share these two fears. They divide, however, on how to deal with them.

Perhaps the Columbine High School incident (see article on pages 23–24) and other incidents like it confirm some people's belief that all or most guns should be outlawed. People holding this opinion may tend to see the government as the friend and protector of the people. They may believe in the principle, announced by political philosophers from Thomas Hobbes to John Locke and John Stuart Mill, that in a civil society people must turn over their personal right of self protection to the government in return for protection by that government from violence, both foreign and domestic. They believe in the stability and permanence of a democratic process in which citizens make law and are effectively protected by it.

Many opponents of gun control, on the other hand, are convinced that if guns are outlawed, all hope is lost, and chaos will rule. These people fear being defenseless in the face of a growing threat from criminals. They even fear being defenseless against the government. Some people feel that the government itself may be our worst enemy. Distrusting the social contract in which people turn over their personal right of self protection, along with their guns, to the government in return for protection from criminals, as well as foreign and domestic violence in general, these people remind us that, in the twentieth century, Stalin, Hitler, and Pol Pot have led nations down paths that America only by the grace of God has thus far failed to tread.

Although some people raise the topic of hunting when the subject of gun control is discussed—i.e., opponents of gun control cite the right to hunt and provide food for oneself and one's family, and advocates of gun control point out that hunters need only to use rifles, not semi-automatic weapons—hunting has relatively little to do with the gun control issue on either side, because only a small minority of people hunt, and only a small minority of people object to hunting. The heart of the issue is actually a matter of what people fear the most—personal harm. Guns are weapons. Whether you advocate a right to bear arms, or a right to be free of people bearing arms, your main concern is the potential of personal harm.

Both proponents of gun control and opponents of gun control like to cite the second amendment to the Constitution, which reads, "A well regulated militia, being necessary to the security of a free state, the right of the people to keep and bear arms shall not be infringed." While gun control opponents underscore the idea that this amendment to the Constitution guarantees the right to bear arms, gun control advocates point out that the context in which this amendment was written no longer applies: Since the formation of the armed forces, the National Guard, and various branches of federal and local law enforcement, the private ownership of guns is no longer our only means of national defense.

The articles on pages 23–39 describe much of the history and the current status of the gun control debate. The first article, as previously noted, is about the Columbine High School incident. The second and third articles discuss the new system of computerized, instant background checks on gun buyers. The fourth article pertains to the issue of a loophole in the Brady gun control law. The fifth article is an editorial about lawsuits against handguns, and the sixth article is about the debate over "smart guns." As you read the articles, attempt to decide what is, for you, the real issue in this gun control controversy.

The New York Times

April 22, 1999

Fifteen Bodies Found
as Police Search Colorado School

By SAM HOWE VERHOVEK

LITTLETON, COLO.—After a long day of agony for victims' parents and anxiety for police officers searching for explosives, the authorities Wednesday evening removed the bodies of 15 people killed in a massacre at Columbine High School on Tuesday.

Among the dead were the two students who are believed to have unleashed the carnage before turning their guns on themselves. They were found shot in the head.

Twelve of the dead, including both suspected gunmen, were found in the school library, said the Jefferson County Sheriff, John Stone. Sheriff Stone said there were so many weapons and explosive devices—including 30 bombs, a semi-automatic rifle and pistol and two shotguns—that investigators were still unsure how the gunmen got it all inside the school....

The incident set off a national bout of soul-searching and debates over whether the killings were spurred by easy access to guns or by the violent images on television and in video games to which American children are routinely exposed. President Clinton said in Washington that "all of us are struggling to understand exactly what happened and why."...

The shootings had immediate political reverberations as well: in Colorado and at least two other states, sponsors of legislation expanding the rights to carry guns or insulating gunmakers from lawsuits withdrew those measures Wednesday....

The repercussions were felt far beyond Colorado.

In Alabama and Florida, the school shooting led lawmakers to postpone consideration of bills that would prohibit cities and counties from suing gun makers for the cost of gun violence. The bills, similar to others passed around the country, were introduced at the behest of the National Rifle Association to protect the firearms industry from liability suits.

Also Wednesday, officials of the N.R.A. said they had decided to scale back their national membership meeting, scheduled for May 1 in Denver.

In a letter, the association's president, the actor Charlton Heston, said the group was canceling a gun show along with all other "festive ceremonies normally associated with our annual gathering." The group was nevertheless going to hold its annual members meeting at the city's convention center.... But Heston and some politicians said that the violence might have been averted if someone else had been armed at the school.

"Had there been someone who was armed, in this particular situation, in my opinion, it may have stabilized," said Gov. Jesse Ventura of Minnesota, who supports loosening restrictions on concealed handguns. "I believe it supports conceal-and-carry because of the fact that what happens when a group of unarmed individuals are confronted with people with weapons like this, you have no defense."

The New York Times

December 6, 1998

Instant Checks on Gun Buyers
Already Paying Off, Clinton Says

By David E. Sanger

WASHINGTON—President Clinton said Saturday that the new system of computerized, instant background checks on gun buyers, run by the FBI, had already stopped "400 felons, fugitives, stalkers and other prohibited purchasers from walking away with new guns."

In his weekly radio address, Clinton also accused the National Rifle Association, which has gone to court to challenge the new instant check system, of trying to "gut the Brady law and undermine our efforts to keep more guns from falling into the wrong hands."

The law, named for James Brady, who was President Ronald Reagan's press secretary until being severely wounded during an assassination attempt on Reagan in 1981, narrowly passed in Congress five years ago.

Until the new check system was put in place last week, gun buyers often had to wait days or weeks for a background check before they could purchase a gun. Under the new system, gun dealers can call a central number for an immediate background check, although some dealers complained last week that they had difficulty reaching operators at the number and in some cases were kept waiting for lengthy periods.

Clinton said Saturday that he would press for further restrictions on gun sales when the new Congress convenes in January.

"One of my top priorities will be to pass legislation to require a minimum waiting period before a handgun sale becomes final," he said, arguing that background checks had to be combined with a "cooling off period" that would stop "rash acts of violence and give authorities more time to stop illegal gun purchases."

He also called for the closing of a loophole in the existing law that allows juveniles convicted of violent crimes to purchase guns once they turn 21 years old. Clinton has asked the Treasury Department and the Justice Department to assure that guns sold at gun shows are not exempt from the background checks.

When the NRA filed its suit earlier last week to block the new instant check system, it argued that the FBI was violating federal laws that forbid the creation of a national register of gun owners.

James Jay Baker, a spokesman for the NRA, said in a statement issued on Tuesday, "The clear intent of the Congress was to conduct the background check unobtrusively at the point of sale, without delay, and with all respect to the privacy of the gun purchaser.

"Unfortunately, that is not what the federal government is doing. Clearly, the attorney general and the Justice Department are in violation of that intent and that law."

Clinton dismissed the NRA's arguments Saturday as a "desperate effort to kill" enforcement of the Brady law.

"We can't turn back," he said. "In these last five years Brady background checks have stopped nearly a quarter of a million illegal handgun sales. We can't go back to the days when dangerous criminals walked away from stores with new guns, no questions asked."

The New York Times

December 1, 1998

New Gun Checks under Fire

By The Associated Press

Waiting to buy shotguns at the Olde English Gun Shoppe didn't anger Bob Niday and Dwayne Petty so much. It was the reason they were waiting.

It took 10 to 15 minutes for shop workers to complete a background check on the two Ohio men Monday. It was the first day for a new federal system that requires the check for all firearms purchases—not just handguns.

"I think it's stupid for the simple reason that robbers and murderers are not going to walk into a gun store and buy a gun," said Niday, 54.

"It's silly to me," added Petty, 27. "It's a way for the government to find out what the honest people have in their homes."

The men waiting in the western Ohio village of Ginghamsburg were among many discontented gun buyers across the nation Monday as technical delays slowed things down.

In Holden, Maine, gun dealer Ralph McLeod said he made 25 calls to the computerized background check system and got constant busy signals Monday morning. A young customer waiting to buy a $225 semiautomatic handgun was turned away as a result.

An estimated 12.4 million firearms are sold each year in the United States. All will be covered by background checks, as will an additional 2.5 million annual transactions when an owner retrieves a firearm from a pawn shop.

The new system is required under the Brady Act, which established federal background checks for handgun purchasers almost five years ago. Now people buying rifles and shotguns must submit to checks, too.

The Justice Department has given states $200 million in the past few years to help them computerize their records. The FBI says that once the system is working smoothly, approvals should take just three minutes.

Activists on both sides of the gun control debate have serious problems with the background checks.

The National Rifle Association filed suit in U.S. District Court in Washington on Friday contending a decision by the Justice Department to maintain a list of all people who apply to buy guns—not just those found to have committed felonies or have other problems in their backgrounds—violates federal law, including the Brady Act.

"This is about privacy and freedom from government snooping in our lives," said Wayne LaPierre, the NRA's executive vice president.

He said the Brady Act requires the government to destroy all records compiled in checking the backgrounds of would-be gun purchasers except those of people found ineligible to own guns. It also prohibits establishing any national gun registry, he said.

And groups like Handgun Control say the new law is too lax because it decreases the time officials have to research a potential buyer. Under the old law, they had as long as five days if they needed it. Under the new law, they have three.

Federal law bans gun purchases by people convicted or under indictment on felony charges, fugitives, the mentally ill, those with dishonorable military discharges, those who have renounced U.S. citizenship, illegal aliens, illegal drug users and those convicted of domestic violence misdemeanors or under domestic violence restraining orders. State laws add other categories.

States had the option of running the system themselves, or having the federal government do it for free. Sixteen states chose to do it themselves; 10 others will run their own handgun checks and let the FBI handle other purchases.

Gun-control activists don't like that 24 states are having the FBI do the background checks for them. Federal officials don't have access to such background information as restraining orders and involuntary commitments to mental hospitals.

James Brady, the former White House spokesman for whom the Brady Law is named, said the lack of access to some background information is a flaw in the law. He and his wife, Sarah, who became gun control activists after he was wounded in the 1981 attempt on President Reagan's life, also said a waiting period should be restored to prevent impulse shootings such as suicides.

Gun dealers say they and their customers were confused by the new system, and many had trouble getting through to the FBI's approval hot line.

"Somewhere late morning or early afternoon, the complete system went down. The phones literally wouldn't answer," said Barry Perry of Perry's Gun Shop in Wendell, N.C. "I don't know if it was a computer overload or too many incoming calls."

The FBI did not respond to requests for an interview.

At Gary's Gun Shop in Sioux Falls, S.D., owner Gary Salmen was planning to put in a third phone line to handle the background-checking calls.

"We're going to end up with one person at least part time spending all their time on the phone," he said.

Others in the gun business said they find the system oppressive, even if it eventually does work smoothly.

"The unfortunate part is it affects the people that probably perhaps it shouldn't affect," said Bill Gleason, a salesman at Dave's Guns in Aurora, Colo. Most people who buy rifles and shotguns are sportsmen and level-headed people—"certainly not criminals."

The New York Times

November 8, 1998

Clinton Calls for Closing
Big Loophole in Gun Law

President Clinton announced today that he had ordered the Treasury and Justice Departments to recommend ways to stop gun shows from exploiting a loophole in the Brady gun control law.

"We didn't fight as hard as we did to pass the Brady law only to let a handful of unscrupulous gun dealers disrespect the law, undermine our progress and put our families at risk," the President said in his weekly radio address. He added that gun shows have become "illegal arms bazaars" for criminals and gun runners.

The President directed Treasury Secretary Robert E. Rubin and Attorney General Janet Reno to present to him within two months a plan to close the Brady law loophole and prohibit any gun sale without a background check.

Mr. Clinton said gun control efforts would also be strengthened on Nov. 30 when the Justice Department begins the National Instant Criminal Background Check System. This system will give law-enforcement officials access to a wider array of records than is now available.

Also, by Nov. 30 the background checks will apply not only to handguns but also to rifles and shotguns and firearms transfers at pawn shops. With that system in place, the number of background checks for gun purchases will increase from an estimated 4 million a year to 12 million, Mr. Clinton said.

The Government estimates that five million people a year attend gun shows, often held in convention centers, school gymnasiums or fairgrounds.

The requirement for waiting periods and background checks does not apply to gun show sales.

The President's message was echoed by Sarah Brady, the wife of the former White House press secretary James S. Brady, who was wounded in the 1981 assassination attempt on former President Ronald Reagan. The law, named in Mr. Brady's honor, established a five-day waiting period for hand gun purchases so that background checks could be performed on buyers.

"In state after state, criminals can now walk into a weekend gun show and buy a gun with no questions asked from an unlicensed dealer that is selling from his or her 'private collection,'" Mrs. Brady, chairwoman of the advocacy group Handgun Control Inc., said in a written statement. "That's an open invitation to criminals."

"The past five years have demonstrated the importance of observing waiting periods and doing background checks at gun stores," she added, "but we now need to extend the Brady law to include all gun sales occurring at gun shows and flea markets."

Mr. Clinton noted that gun shows are popular in his home state of Arkansas, which he visited on Friday after taping his radio address at the White House. "I have visited and enjoyed them over the years," he said. "They're often the first place parents teach their children how to handle firearms safely.

"But at too many guns shows, a different, dangerous trend is emerging. Some of these gun shows have become illegal arms bazaars for criminals and gun traffickers to buy and sell guns on a cash-and-carry, no-questions-asked basis."

Mr. Clinton noted that Florida voters passed a measure on Tuesday to enable communities to require background checks for the public sale of all guns.

"I believe this should be the law of the land: no background check, no gun, no exceptions," he said.

The New York Times

November 14, 1998

Lawsuits against Handguns

EDITORIAL DESK

Chicago has now joined New Orleans in a promising new legal offensive against gun violence. On Thursday, Chicago's Mayor, Richard Daley, filed a $433 million lawsuit against 22 gun manufacturers, 4 gun distributors and 12 suburban stores. The suit charged them with creating a "public nuisance" by knowingly flooding the city, which has some of the nation's strictest gun control laws, with illegal weapons.

Chicago's lawsuit follows by just two weeks a related legal action against the gun industry filed by New Orleans, based on different legal grounds. The purpose of both suits, as well as stepped-up litigation by individuals against gun makers, is to force a recalcitrant industry to make its deadly product less accessible to criminals and children. Spokesmen for the gun industry deny responsibility for gun violence and deride the suits as a far-fetched attempt to duplicate the success of the anti-tobacco litigation. They also threaten to use their political muscle if, as expected, Philadelphia and other big cities follow up with their own lawsuits—overlooking the strong support for gun control among voters. But as a legal matter, the weapons makers have good reason to be worried.

No one can say how the courts will respond to the central premise of the Chicago case—that gun manufacturers intentionally saturate gun stores just outside city limits with more guns than the lawful market could possibly absorb, in order to supply a large and profitable illegal market. But judges and juries are aware that gun violence imposes heavy costs on urban America. They are also likely to be impressed by evidence produced by undercover operatives that criminals can easily buy guns at suburban stores to use for criminal acts inside the Chicago city limits. Laurence Tribe, a Harvard Law School professor who helped prepare some of the successful litigation against the tobacco industry, suggests that the manufacturers' argument that they are several steps removed from the actual sale of guns may not be enough to escape liability.

The suit filed by the Mayor of New Orleans, Marc Morial, takes a different legal approach, using the traditional claim of product liability to try to hold the gun industry accountable. By failing to incorporate feasible safety devices, Mr. Morial argues, firearms manufacturers have made their product "unreasonably dangerous." The idea that a manufacturer's responsibility extends beyond the gun's owner and intended users to unintended users, like children, gives the case a certain novelty. But the principle that a manufacturer can be held liable for damage caused by a product that is "unreasonably dangerous" is solidly imbedded in Louisiana law.

The technology exists to make guns safer and to "personalize" a weapon so that only its owner can fire it—by, for instance, installing a simple combination lock. It should not be necessary to sue the industry to force it to meet its obligations. But so far nothing else has worked.

The New York Times

October 22, 1998

"Smart Guns" Setting Off Debate: How Smart Will They Really Be?

By Iver Peterson

The 9-millimeter semiautomatic looks like an ordinary pistol, evil and menacing to gun haters, strangely beautiful to gun fanciers. But it is no ordinary weapon; pull the trigger and nothing happens.

Only when a shooter puts on a special wristband, containing a tiny radio transmitter, does a squeeze of the trigger make the hammer snap down hard, making the gun every bit the lethal weapon it appears to be. The pistol is a computerized "smart gun," designed to fire only for its owner. And its maker, Colt's Manufacturing Company, sees it as the firearms industry's reply to one of the strongest criticisms of gun control advocates—that guns too often fall into the wrong hands, those of children or criminals, usually with horrible consequences.

Colt's hopes, naturally, that the new product will help it survive what has become a long decline in the gun market. But in a broader sense, company executives and other believers in the smart-gun concept say they also hope that it will redefine the gun debate in America, and narrow the bitter gulf between those who see evil in guns and those who see good.

A smart gun is still at least a year from coming to market, but already several states, including New Jersey and Maryland, are considering legislation that would require recognition technology in guns sold there. And though the political battle is only now warming up, unusual alliances are being struck.

Some gun manufacturers, like Sturm, Ruger & Company, are openly skeptical about smart guns, saying that the technology is not reliable enough. And some ardent gun foes would rather abolish handgun sales altogether. But at the same time, Colt's has found a supporter in Handgun Control Inc., the chief gun-control lobby in Washington, led by Sarah Brady, whose husband, James S. Brady, was gravely wounded in the assassination attempt on President Ronald Reagan in 1981.

"The only people who oppose or question the usefulness of developing smart guns are the extremists at both ends of the gun control debate," said Naomi Paiss, the group's communications director. "Gun manufacturers who are not investing in smart gun technology are obviously quite afraid that their wares will instantly become the Ford Pintos of the 90s."

"On the other side there are the extremists—I don't think it is unfair to describe them that way—who oppose making safer guns because they really believe that no gun should be sold or privately owned in this country. They are both wrong."

Several other companies are pursuing different smart-gun technologies, including one that depends on recognizing a gun owner's fingerprints, and another that recognizes the owner's hand size. The Colt gun is the closest to production, however.

Colt's built its smart gun prototype with the help of a $500,000 research grant from the National Institute of Justice, a Federal agency, but it spent millions more on the research, said Marc Fontaine, Colt's chief operating officer. Colt's lineup of semiautomatic handguns range[s] in price at retail from about $250 for a light, .22-caliber target pistol to $813 for its new .45-caliber Combat Commander. The recognition technology will add $300 to $400 to the price of each gun, Mr. Fontaine said.

There is no denying that U.S. gun sales, and particularly handgun sales, have been slipping steadily over the last two decades. American firearms production has declined to 3.8 million in 1996 from 5 million in 1977 and handgun production to 1.5 million from 1.9 million in the same period.

To the executives at Colt's, which has only recently emerged from bankruptcy and expects this year to turn its first profit in 12 years, the smart gun promises to win new markets, particularly among women, a small but growing segment of gun owners who may see a smart gun as a solution to their fear of having their own weapon used against them.

"Everybody is going to want smart guns," said Buck Hendrickson, a Colt's vice president. "Then the little kids can't shoot each other and nobody can take a police officer's gun away from him and shoot him, and states like New Jersey and New York and Maryland and Delaware and maybe even Virginia are going to have legislatures saying, 'The only kind of gun you can buy here is a smart gun.'"

Steven M. Sliwa, Colt's president, called the smart gun a "major growth prospect" for Colt's.

But David M. Guthrie, director of equity research at the Memphis investment firm of Morgan Keegan & Company, said the smart gun would only sell if the law commanded it.

"People that buy guns tend to be pretty conservative and they don't like things that are far out," Mr. Guthrie said. "You might sell a smart gun to someone who wants a gun for self-defense, but unless there is some type of forced legislation that gives you no choice, people are not going to gravitate to a product like this." Morgan, Keegan has underwritten stock offerings for Sturm, Ruger, the country's only major firearms manufacturer that is publicly held.

However far it is from production or widespread acceptance, the new "safe gun" or "personalized gun," as it is also known, is still the biggest news in years to come out of the firearms industry, which has been rooted here in the Connecticut River Valley since Samuel Colt began making revolvers more than 160 years ago.

In fact, the smart gun is the first technological countermeasure the gun industry has mounted to the wave of legal and marketplace challenges that have confronted the industry in recent decades—from laws against assault-style rifles to recent efforts by anti-gun forces to use product liability lessons of the tobacco wars against gun makers.

But while Colt's officials are enthusiastic about the gun's prospects, critics inside and outside the industry see it as a waste of time.

Smith & Wesson, Colt's big rival a few miles to the north in Springfield, Mass., suspended its smart gun program some time ago to wait for the technology to advance. L. E. Shultz, president and chief executive at Smith & Wesson, echoes the main argument against smart guns, that technology will do nothing to stop the misuse of guns by their proper owners.

"If you want to shoot your wife, you will go out and get your gun and shoot her," Mr. Shultz said. "It's the aura of the smart gun as the solution to that situation that I have a problem with, because I don't think we will be able to develop in our lifetime or even in our children's lifetime a gun that can determine its user's attitude."

Sturm, Ruger, based in Southport, Conn., has also rejected the current leading technology for the smart gun: the radio transmitter, called a transponder, which, when brought close to the gun, engages its firing system.

"The major failure that we see with any of these so-called smart guns is the battery," said Stephen L. Sanetti, vice president and general counsel at Ruger, which is the only publicly held American firearms company. "Whether you are on a target range or on a hunting trip you saved for for years, or, in the worst-case scenario, defending your family, if the battery has failed, your options are that either the gun doesn't work or the safety doesn't work, and that makes the technology incompatible with firearms.

"Because one of the major components of the safety of a firearm is its reliability under all conditions."

A safe gun would also continue to work if its transmitter bracelet were stolen along with the weapon, as well as if, in a struggle with an assailant, the gun were fired while still in or touching the owner's hand. The Colt's smart gun's police transponder will be programmable so that officers can fire one another's guns.

Testing to Satisfy Police Officers

Colt's officials say that their smart-gun prototype still has to undergo real-life testing—dropping it in the mud and hard surfaces, using it in the rain—before it will be ready to go on the market. The testing will be intended to satisfy police officers, who are expected to be the first users of the guns; 13 percent of officers killed in the line of duty are shot by their own guns.

The transponder used by Colt's has a range of only a few inches, Colt's officials said, making a gun useless even if held within feet of an officer by an assailant. Use by the police would go a long way to reassuring civilian customers that the smart gun will fire when it should, Colt's officials believe.

But it is the unproven nature of the smart gun that causes the lobbying arm of the National Rifle Association, the country's largest gun owners' group, to resist any laws mandating their adoption, said James Jay Baker, the N.R.A.'s executive director.

"I don't think there is any harm in proceeding with the development of a safer firearm," he said, "but I think there is a problem with adopting a technology that doesn't even exist yet. Some of the anti-gun proponents in Congress are already talking about mandating it for everybody, and it's not even on the market yet, and the police haven't even accepted the technology yet."

Researchers Concerned about Battery Life

Sandia National Laboratories in Albuquerque, N.M., a Federal research center, issued a 172-page review of smart gun technology for use in police work in 1996 with a highly iffy conclusion. After reviewing more than a dozen possible technologies, from Colt's radio frequency tag system to biometric devices that cause the gun to recognize, say, the length of a particular police officer's finger, it found that no approach scored higher than a B, in part because of concerns about battery life.

"It may take a generation of smart gun systems to come and go before a smart gun is not only common, but favored over a non-smart gun," the report, by D. R. Weiss, concluded.

In a telephone interview, Mr. Weiss predicted that smart guns would eventually be perfected, but he cautioned that the technology should be settled before laws mandating them are enacted.

"I think we will see them eventually," he said, "but we will have to make sure that the job is done properly, because it would be very detrimental if something were put out and widely distributed and it didn't work. The mistake could cost smart guns their reputation."

Outside the gun industry, the smart gun has provoked conflicting reactions. Mr. Brady, the former White House press secretary, went to Trenton in September to endorse New Jersey's proposed smart-gun legislation, which is strongly opposed by the N.R.A. and by New Jersey's influential gun-owners lobby, the Coalition of New Jersey Sportsmen. (Although the the New Jersey legislation is supported by some members of both parties, it faces steep obstacles in getting to the floors of the House and Senate.)

But the more stringently anti-gun Violence Policy Center, which favors phasing out private handgun ownership entirely, opposes them. The center maintains that smart guns are unlikely to reduce suicides, the largest single cause of death from guns, and that the second-highest category, homicides, are most often committed among acquaintances.

Moreover, the center maintains, most gun owners have more than one handgun, leaving plenty of "dumb" guns still at large.

Finally, the Center objects to any technology that is likely to lead to increased handgun sales—and additional sales are just what Mr. Hendrickson at Colt's expects to get from smart guns.

"Let's just say this thing hits next year and it works, and it works well," Mr. Hendrickson said. "You're going to see so much legislation that says that only the smart gun can be sold that it's going to put the other gun factories out of business."

QUESTIONS FOR CLASS DISCUSSION OR DEBATE

As you conduct further research on gun control and the right to bear arms, many questions may come to your mind. If you plan to debate these issues in class, you may want to consider arguing positions related to the following statements:

- The constitution guarantees the right to own handguns.
- The constitution guarantees the right to own automatic weapons.
- Guns don't kill people, people do.
- Armed citizens are safer than unarmed citizens.
- Moses would have carried a gun if it had been available to him.

RESOURCES FOR CLASS DEBATES AND FURTHER STUDY

GUN CONTROL ON THE INTERNET

For further information about gun control, you may want to explore the following internet sites:

Statistics from many U.S. government agencies, including crime and
   weapons data
   www.fedstats.gov
The National Rifle Association
   www.nra.org
The Citizens Committee for the Right to Keep and Bear Arms
   www.ccrkba.org
Gun Owners of America
   www.gunowners.org
Handgun Control, Inc. (HCI)
   www.handguncontrol.org
The Coalition to Stop Gun Violence (CSGV)
   www.gunfree.org/csgv
Violence Policy Center
   www.vpc.org

FURTHER REFERENCE

Bijlefeld, Marjohn. *The Gun Control Debate: A Documentary History.* Greenwood Publishing Group. 1997.
Bruce, John M., and Clyde Wilcox, eds. *The Changing Politics of Gun Control.* Rowan & Littlefield. 1998.

Carter, Gregg Lee. *Gun Control Movement*. Macmillan Publishing Company. 1997.

Cottrol, Robert J., ed. *Gun Control and the Constitution: Sources and Explorations on the Second Amendment*. Garland Publishing. 1994.

LaRosa, Benedict D. *Gun Control: A Historical Perspective*. Candlestick Publishing. 1996.

Levine, Herbert M. *Gun Control*. Raintree. 1997.

3

IMMIGRATION

C onsider the graph below. It indicates that immigration to the United
   States reached its first peak in the decades before and after 1910, and
that since a sharp downturn during World War II, immigration has climbed
each decade to numbers that now nearly equal the great pre-World War I
migrant inflow.

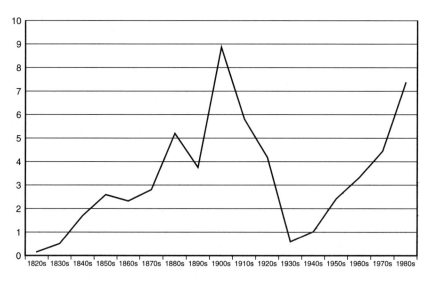

U.S. Immigration by Decade 1820–1990 in Millions

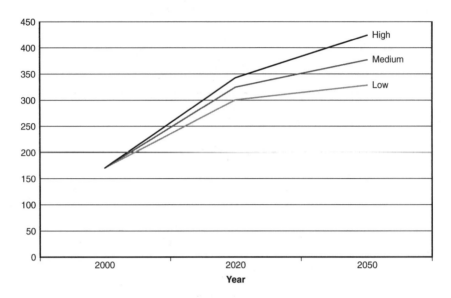

Population Projections in Millions

By the end of the 1990s, immigrants will have added nearly ten million people to the U.S. general population, which, by 2000, will be approximately 270 million. How fast will the U.S. population grow if current trends continue? As illustrated in the graph above, the U.S. Census bureau provides three sets of projections, based on varying premises that yield low, medium, or high rates of growth in the coming years.

If we assume that immigration continues from 2000 to 2050 at the rate of ten million immigrants per decade, and that the general population in 2050 will be 383 million, then new immigrants will make up 24 percent of the *increase* in U.S. population between now and 2050. What kinds of people will these new immigrants be? Let's look first at where they will come from, assuming they are similar to those who came here from 1961 to 1993. As the chart at the top of page 45 indicates, about half of the immigrants currently coming to the United States are from either Mexico or Asia. Europe, which supplied so many immigrants at the beginning of the twentieth century, will provide an increasingly smaller share of this country's new residents. The apprehension that is generated when people from a different culture come to live in our states and neighborhoods is part of what is behind the immigration controversy. Apprehension is further heightened by fear that new immigrants will take jobs from people already here. The traditional pattern of immigrant employment is that newcomers most often first take the menial and low-paying jobs in society, and later move into more lucrative occupations. Many of today's immigrants, however, more quickly than in the past, assume occupations with high levels of responsibility and compensation.

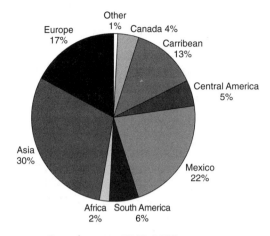

Immigrants 1961–1993

As the chart below illustrates, the immigrants of the first half of the twenty-first century will hold occupations similar to those of the general American population.

The following *New York Times* articles (on pages 47–58) present a summary of some of the key issues in the immigration controversy. The first article takes a side in the debate over the desirability of slowing the flow of immigrants to the United States. This article is followed by two additional articles, the first of which summarizes recent actions related to immigration in Congress, and the second of which describes some of the problems faced by new immigrants. As you read these articles, identify what you believe to be the real issues.

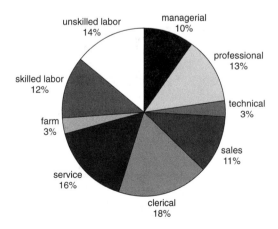

Immigrant Occupations

The New York Times

March 9, 1998

Immigrants Aren't the Problem: We Are

By Bill McKibben

In the next few weeks, the half million members of the Sierra Club will vote to set the club's policy on the issue of immigration. Since the Sierra Club does not exactly control Congress, the final count won't much matter, but the debate, which has already been spirited, represents an invaluable chance to raise the issue of how many people this country can and should contain.

Immigration is about as difficult a moral subject as one can imagine, so even the proposed change in Sierra Club policy—in favor of an unspecified "reduction in net immigration"—has ignited controversy. In a world of desperate poverty, it is hard for citizens of the richest nation to argue that the door should be closed, especially since nearly all of us can recall our immigrant roots.

Not only that, too many people who support tighter controls on immigration are racists of various types. I got a letter last month from a board member of one national group working on population issues in which he complained about "barbarians" who littered the subways and played "ugly" music. (He professed to prefer that all-American composer J. S. Bach.) So it is no surprise that most wise people, including most wise environmentalists, simply ignore the matter: Currently, the official Sierra Club policy is to "take no position on immigration levels or on policies governing immigration into the United States."

Environmentalists have focused on living more simply and more efficiently as the keys to our problems here at home, but many, myself included, have largely overlooked the messier and more divisive question of our sheer numbers. While our birth rate is just below the replacement level of 2.1—the number of children each mother would need to bear to keep the population constant—our total population continues to grow quickly compared with that of other developed nations. Part of this is because of our longer life spans and the echoes of the baby-boom bulge—even at two children apiece, we'll be living longer life spans and the echoes of the baby-boom bulge—even at two children apiece, we'll be increasing our numbers for decades to come. But our population is also growing because we have by far the world's highest level of immigration—something like 800,000 legal immigrants take up residence here each year (not to mention illegal immigrants, estimated at 300,000 a year). Natural increase and immigration, the Census Bureau projects, may combine to swell our population by as much as 50 percent in the next 50 years, bringing it to nearly 400 million; by even the most conservative estimates, there will be 30 percent more Americans by the middle of the next century.

That's a problem for two reasons. The first, and most obvious, is that this country, so seemingly empty when Europeans initially arrived, is by some definitions becoming crowded. It's true that the Plains remain sparsely populated, and probably always will. But the places Americans want to live are jammed. The Northeast corridor of suburbs and cities is already more densely populated than Haiti or El Salvador; California's 30 million may become 50 million by 2050. With each year, the ring of suburbs spreads a little farther out, the roads become a bit more crowded, the margin for wildlife becomes slightly smaller. That endless growth places real stress on our supplies of everything from water to silence, from farmland to solitude. Such growth even strains our democracy. When the Constitution was ratified, each member of Congress represented 30,000 voters; now it's 570,000.

But there's a bigger problem still. Americans, as the world's most voracious consumers, contribute far more per capita to the world's environmental problems than anyone else. So an extra hundred million Americans means, for instance, a staggering amount of carbon dioxide entering the atmosphere and warming the climate. It's true that we could alleviate some of that problem if each of us consumed less and consumed more efficiently—if we lived in smaller homes heated by the sun. I've spent most of my career writing about just such ideas, and believe in them wholeheartedly.

But at the moment, we're building bigger homes and driving bigger cars. And even if we came to our senses, the momentum of natural increase and immigration would render most of our changes meaningless. As the President's Council on Sustainable Development pointed out in 1996, domestic population growth means we'll need to increase our energy efficiency 50 percent in the next half century just to run in place.

This is a very different argument from the traditional "they'll-take-our-jobs-from-us" lament. Economists by now have mostly concluded that immigrants actually create wealth, which should come as no surprise to anyone who has visited Brooklyn or Queens in recent years. If those who wanted to immigrate here stayed instead in Juarez or Shanghai or, for that matter, Dublin, they would do far less damage to the planet precisely because they would not be as rich. That's the point, and that's also the rub. People want to come here for a better life with more opportunities, and who are we to deny them that chance?

We of course already deny plenty of people that chance—even our current, historically generous immigration ceiling means many people aren't allowed in. Of the world's huddled masses, only the tiniest fraction will ever come here even with existing laws. And while some population-control advocates want to see immigration all but stopped, most whom I've talked to would prefer to see the limits cut roughly in half, to about 400,000 annually, with special provisions for asylum seekers. At that rate, if our birth rate simultaneously fell to the European average of 1.5 children, we could see our population stop growing within a generation.

Still, such a policy would be harsh. It would mean 400,000 more people a year who would be turned away at the door—people with particular hopes, particular sorrows. And all in the name of as-yet fairly abstract problems like global warming. Such restrictions would come at real cost to the American dream, too; in most cities I know, New York included, immigrants best exemplify the kind of citizenship and community spirit increasingly absent from the nation's mainstream.

So I think we have no right to pass such laws, or even to support them in nonbinding forms like Sierra Club referendums, unless we also take serious steps in our own lives to lessen our impact on the environment. If we're not willing to reduce the size of our families or the size of our sport utility vehicles, then cutting immigration is piggish scapegoating; it may save some of our landscape, but at the price of our national soul. If, however, we are willing to take some painful steps ourselves, then we earn the right to tell some tough truths to others—chief among them that even this rich land can't grow forever. Numbers count.

The New York Times

November 1, 1998

The 1998 Campaign: Immigrants; Once Divisive, Immigration Now a Muted Issue

By Mirta Ojito

TIt is the weekend before the elections, and immigration, the source of much national angst in years past, has disappeared from the election debate, although not from lawmakers' political agendas.

In the past year or so, while the nation has focused on the White House and Wall Street, Congress has quietly scaled back some provisions of several 1996 laws that were written to discourage immigration by cutting a range of benefits to legal residents and stepping up deportation efforts. The moves, capped by pro-immigration provisions in this year's budget bill, signal lawmakers' awareness of the growing voting power of immigrants.

"A couple of years ago people were advocating to build a wall around the country," said Senator Spencer Abraham, a Michigan Republican who introduced several pro-immigration provisions in this year's spending bill. "That's no longer the case. Before, we had heard only one side of the immigration issue. Now, we get to talk about some of the positive contributions immigrants have made."

The immigration measures in the budget bill that President Clinton signed—allowing almost 50,000 Haitian refugees to stay in the country, for example, and increasing the number of visas granted to foreign professionals—would have been unthinkable four years ago, when anti-immigration themes dominated political campaigns nationally, or two years ago, when Congress passed what many consider the most anti-immigrant legislation in decades.

No one is suggesting that Congress is dismantling those laws, particularly the Illegal Immigration Reform and Immigrant Responsibility Act of 1996. Indeed, now that the Immigration and Naturalization Service is flush with money, most of the harsher measures of that law are being enforced.

Still, there seems to be a growing consensus among lawmakers that too much control of immigration is not good—for politicians, who recognize that immigrants' votes could be pivotal in some races; for businesses and the economy, because valued employees have had to return home and prospective hires have not been granted visas, or even for the Government itself, since control is expensive and time consuming.

Those assumptions, coupled with good economic news, have led some anti-immigration members of Congress to take a cautious approach to immigration issues or ignore them.

"The Republicans are taking a wait-and-see attitude," said Representative Luis Gutierrez, an Illinois Democrat who is pro-immigration. "They don't want to offend one side or alienate the other."

Among some lawmakers, especially those who advocate a hard line against immigrants, there is a sense that the laws of 1996 were so sweeping that very little more can be done or added to the debate. The budget for the Immigration and Naturalization Service, much of it dedicated to enforcement, now surpasses that of the F.B.I., and the agency has more employees than either the Department of State or Labor.

"The Clinton Administration took some major steps showing that it was serious in trying to control illegal immigration," said T. Alexander Aleinikoff, a law professor at Georgetown University and former general counsel and associate commissioner of the immigration service. "Some people are saying, 'We've dealt with the problem. We've done what we can. Let's move on.'"

But the issue of illegal immigration is far from resolved, Mr. Aleinikoff said. There are about five million such immigrants in the United States and no law that specifically addresses what to do with them.

Instead, lawmakers are sidestepping immigration in their campaigns, and have been passing legislation that benefits immigrants and, in some cases, reverses aspects of previous laws.

Congress has restored most of the welfare benefits it took away from legal immigrants in 1996. Lawmakers also restored some of the protections that Central American immigrants had lost, therefore sparing them from deportation. Congress granted amnesty to 150,000 Nicaraguans, 5,000 Cubans and 49,700 Haitians and allowed hundreds of thousands of illegal immigrants who hope to gain permanent visas to stay in the United States instead of having to go home to file their applications, as the 1996 law dictated.

Congress granted $171 million to the immigration agency to speed the naturalization process and, for the first time in years, it increased by 5,000 the number of refugees allowed into the country every year.

"The pendulum is definitely swinging our way," said Judith E. Golub, director of advocacy for the American Immigration Lawyers Association in Washington.

Advocates for immigrants as well as those who oppose immigration say the pendulum began to swing in favor of immigrants four years ago.

The re-election of California's Governor, Pete Wilson, who won in part by making his anti-immigration platform part of the national debate, was a signal to immigrants everywhere that unless they quickly became U.S. citizens, they too would feel the impact of measures like Proposition 187. The proposition is a California ballot initiative seeking to deny education, health and other benefits to illegal immigrants.

Many rushed to naturalize and thousands of new citizens were ready to vote in the 1996 races. The results caught the Republicans by surprise. In California a newcomer to politics, Loretta Sanchez, a Democrat, unseated the Republican incumbent, Representative Robert K. Dornan.

"Pete Wilson brought out the angry white male in California and used immigration as a hot-button issue to get re-elected," said Frank Sharry, executive director of the National Immigration Forum. "That brought out the angry new citizen in record numbers to vote and punish the Republican Party."

Shortly afterward, Republicans began to change their tune.

Speaker Newt Gingrich set the tone by pledging that his party would reach out to Hispanic people and members of other minorities. He hired an aide to oversee this effort and his office began releasing information translated into Spanish.

And now, running hard against Ms. Sanchez again, Mr. Dornan is calling himself a friend of Hispanic immigrants. In Texas, Gov. George W. Bush, a Republican popular with Hispanic immigrants who is seeking re-election, is spending more money to attract Hispanic voters than any other politician ever, his campaign advisers said.

Advocates for immigrants point to Senator Abraham's appointment as the chairman of the Senate subcommittee on immigration as a turning point. He replaced Senator Alan Simpson, a Republican from Wyoming, who retired two years ago.

With Representative Lamar Smith, a Republican from Texas, Mr. Simpson was the architect of some of the more restrictive of the 1996 anti-immigration laws. Mr. Simpson did not return phone calls.

Mr. Smith, chairman of the House immigration subcommittee, said in a statement: "The passage of a Haitian amnesty reflects year-end budget deal making and not any change of heart in Congress. There was little support in the House for amnesty because it will set a bad precedent and undermines longstanding immigration policy."

The New York Times

April 7, 1998

A Long Wait on the Doorstep:
At Immigration Offices, amid Lines
and Lost Time, an Old Hope Survives

BY MIRTA OJITO

This is where the American dream can seem both closer than ever and impossibly out of reach—in the endless, exhausting lines that form every day before dawn outside the doors of immigration offices.

It is where Esteban Travieso, an immigrant from Uruguay, waited for five and a half hours last week, in line at the immigration office in lower Manhattan to ask how he could replace his lost residency card. Where Geordany Josselin, 21, a Haitian, waited for more than six hours to find out what had happened to his residency application. And where Dora Bintimilla waited for four hours to see how she could bring her daughter from Ecuador so they can be together again after 13 years.

"I have put off coming down here for as much as I could—wouldn't you?" said Mr. Travieso, 27, a truck driver who lives in Queens, pointing to the line stretching behind him. "Everybody here wants the same thing, peace of mind. But to get it, you have to go through hell and back. And, of course, the line."

Despite recent efforts by the Federal Immigration and Naturalization Service to cut down on the need to wait in line for routine services and queries, the waiting persists, not only in New York but also in Newark, Houston, Los Angeles, Miami and other cities with large immigrant populations.

The busiest offices, like the one in lower Manhattan, see an average of 1,000 people a day, and an average wait can be as much as three hours or more. When it is finally their turn, they often encounter surly, uninterested or overburdened workers, who hand them yet another form and tell them to stand in yet another line, or to return another day.

While frustrating encounters with bureaucracy are not a complaint unique to immigrants—as anyone who has visited a motor vehicles office can attest—the burden can be particularly heavy for newcomers. They often have unstable jobs with no vacation time and little flexibility, so taking time off is a hardship. And many immigrants with little education and no English find themselves baffled by the complexity of immigration rules that can determine their future.

Recent changes in immigration laws, which seem to create new deadlines every few months, can make the lines even longer, as misinformed and desperate immigrants flock to offices seeking help.

Ibrahim, 24, a native of Somalia who did not want to reveal his last name, woke up at 4 A.M. on March 30 and rushed to the immigration office in Newark. Another immigrant at the construction site where he works had alerted him to a new deadline for applicants for political asylum. Under a 1996 law, all immigrants who arrived in the United States before April 1, 1997, had until April 1, 1998, to file claims for asylum.

At the same time, and on the same day, another deadline sent another category of immigrants scrambling for help. Under the new law, people who have been in the country illegally for more than a year were required to return to their home countries before April 1 to avoid being barred from re-entering the United States legally for 10 years.

Ibrahim, who left his country in 1996 and now lives in Rahway, N.J., said immigration officials would grant him asylum right away, without forcing him to stand in line or submit to an interview, if only they could see his scars.

"Look at this," he said, lifting his shirt in front of the crowd of onlookers to expose jagged scars inflicted in Somalia and running across his chest. "Is this enough to let me live in America, you think?"

As it turned out, he was in the wrong line. After a two-hour wait, an officer told him that asylum applicants need not show up in person. They must file by mail. Ibrahim left as bewildered as when he arrived.

"I don't know what happens to me now," he said, shrugging off the idea of hiring a lawyer. "I have lived long enough here without one. Maybe I don't need help."

Even without the urgency of an approaching deadline, the lines in front of immigration offices are fed every day by thousands of people puzzled by mind-numbing immigration regulations and motivated by an intense desire to become Americans.

"In the harshest day of winter, there is a line," Alan Atkinson, a spokesman at the local immigration office in New York, said last week. "In the hottest day of the summer, there is a line. In the prettiest day of spring, there is a line. It just never changes."

The lower Manhattan office is the only one for general immigration cases in New York City. In 19 working days in February, it served 10,000 people who walked in with inquiries and 11,500 who came in to file applications for various benefits, Mr. Atkinson said. Rob Koon, a spokesman with the Immigration and Naturalization Service in Washington, said last week that from October of last year until the end of February, at least 2.2 million people went to 79 immigration offices asking for help.

No matter how long the lines seem, though, immigrants agree that the situation is actually better than it was a few years ago.

In New York, people now wait their turn inside a portable structure that protects them from the rain or cold. In Newark, officers regularly canvass the lines trying to spot people who are misinformed and waiting in vain. And in Miami, people are now guaranteed service if they are in line before noon, whereas before, they could wait for hours only to be told at the end of the day that the office was closed.

In addition, the Immigration and Naturalization Service has come up with a range of services—from a web site to satellite offices dedicated to citizenship applications only—to reduce the volume of work at the district offices and, therefore, the waiting time.

Eric Andrus, a spokesman for the agency in Washington, said it now has an automated toll-free number for information and another to request forms. A new line, on which callers can speak to a person, was recently installed, but only for the East Coast; it will be available nationwide in the summer, he said. Citizenship forms are available on the Internet.

"We are not where we want to be yet, but we are trying to make the process more convenient for all," Mr. Andrus said.

In addition, immigration officials recently presented Congress a proposal to separate the enforcement division from the agency's customer service operation. "We could then retrain our officers and offer better service, something advocates for immigrants have been asking us to do for a long time," Mr. Andrus said.

Despite the changes, immigrants and their relatives continue to stand in line because, in many cases, they have no choice. Often, they are poor and illiterate in English and have no access to a computer. Many cannot afford a lawyer but are stymied by long, detailed forms. When they call the information lines, the wait is long and the maze of alternatives so confusing and impersonal that many people prefer to stand in line. They view the line as a necessary evil, one more step in the tangled and expensive process of trying to settle, legally, in the United States.

"You don't call," said Angie Zapitero, 27, who was standing in line in Houston to renew her Mexican husband's work permit. "It's better just to come down here and talk to them. It's faster. You'll be put on hold for hours if you call."

Ivo Dimov, 33, a Bulgarian immigrant, waited outside the immigration offices in Los Angeles with his wife, Tanya, to get a special travel permit for a visit home. Since they arrived six years ago, they have lost an uncle, an aunt, a grandmother and a grandfather, and they want to go back to pay their last respects.

After two hours, they moved inside the building where, after another short line, they were assigned a number and told to wait some more. With about 50 people ahead of them, they were sitting quietly when a woman's shriek from a window caught everybody's attention. "Don't you have any decency here? You treat people like cattle."

The Dimovs appeared resigned. "It's a whole wasted day," he said. "I [don't] even know if I will get what we're here for."

The answers that wait at the end of the long lines can shape the course of a whole life. They can determine whether an immigrant becomes a legal resident or stays underground, learns English or remains illiterate, receives welfare benefits or peddles trinkets in the streets, travels home to see his family or spends his salary on weekly phone calls.

Mr. Josselin, who came to New York from Haiti in 1989, was the first in line on March 30 at the New York immigration office, arriving at 3 A.M. so he would not have to miss much time at work. He hopes to study engineering but needs financial aid, and to get it he has to become a permanent resident. After he applied for a green card, he received a letter advising him that one of his forms was missing.

The immigration officer who dealt with him when his number was called at 7:50 A.M. did not know that Mr. Josselin felt his future was at stake. The officer took her time, unwrapping a piece of gum and carefully placing it in her mouth before she turned to him, without a greeting. Mr. Josselin showed her the letter. She punched his name into her computer and told him she thought his case had been closed and that he needed to reapply.

Mr. Josselin seemed numb throughout the process. He simply moved from line to line, floor to floor, officer to officer and did as he was told, asking few questions. He stood in line again to get some forms for a friend. At 9:15 A.M., six hours and 15 minutes after he started the line, he walked out of the building.

"I have been through this line before," he said. "And I'll do it again if I have to."

QUESTIONS FOR CLASS DISCUSSION OR DEBATE

As you conduct further research on immigration, many questions may come to your mind. If you plan to debate these issues in class, you may want to consider arguing positions related to the following statements:

- Immigrants contribute more than they take from society.
- Morality requires admitting as many immigrants as possible.
- Immigrants take jobs away from Americans.
- America should admit only immigrants who supply skills needed by American business.
- America should always be a melting pot.

RESOURCES FOR CLASS DEBATES AND FURTHER STUDY

IMMIGRATION ON THE INTERNET

In the address box on your web browser, type the following address:

http://search.nytimes.com/search/daily/bin/fastweb?getdoc+site+site
+15227+23+wAAA+immigration

Here you will find a list, prepared by the *New York Times*, of web sites related to the immigration controversy. The materials that may be found on that page appear below.

The *New York Times*

Taking in the Sites/By Jacqueline Savaiano

Despite recent anti-immigration laws and sentiment, legal newcomers can more quickly and easily negotiate the roadblocks. Some World Wide Web sites prepare the user for various bureaucratic immigration processes. In addition, there are sites run by ethnic groups with leads on jobs, recreation, schooling, local clubs and legal issues.

To bone up on how to enter America, work or become a citizen, a first step would be to explore four no-frills sites: those maintained by the *U.S. Immigration and Naturalization Service*, the *State Department*, the *American Immigration Center* and by *Immigration Lawyers on the Web*. These are efficient, cheap alternatives to being kept on hold by the INS or to racking up phone bills looking for immigration lawyers.

The State Department page provides a series of links under the "Visa" heading offering information on the legal requirements for various types of visas, from those available to family members of U.S. citizens to those for specialized workers. Texts of the most recent revisions of basic immigration laws are also available through hyperlinks from this page.

The key link on the INS home page is Frequently Asked Questions, with sublinks like citizenship, green cards, visas, naturalization and residency. Just click in for answers. Under Asylum, for instance, there are details on timing, forms and where to submit them.

The Immigration Service site outlines processes only. For forms or assistance, tap into the sites of the American Immigration Center and Immigration Lawyers on the Web. Under Immigrant Document Preparation, the for-profit American Immigration Center site offers instructions on how to prepare documents from citizenship to replacement of a lost green card, and offers to type and file to the INS for a fee.

For free forms, however, click on What's New at the Immigration Lawyers on the Web home page. Forms will be mailed to visitors within two days.

James Acoba, a Los Angeles immigration lawyer, raises some red flags about these sites. Some information could be inaccurate because of changes in the laws, he said. In addition, look for disclaimers pointing out that the content is not legal advice. See if the information source is regulated.

The bottom line when going through the immigration process? "Find a good lawyer," Acoba said, noting the Law Firms section on the Immigration Lawyers site. To move through the Searchable Lawyer Data Base, type in the area of interest (visa, let's say), language (Spanish) and location (New York City), and specific names pop up. One can partly review credentials using the Full Text Searchable Index, which screens individual lawyers' web sites.

Immigrants can use the growing number of Internet search engines for sites by ethnic groups devoted to the particular cultural and legal needs of new Americans.

A page that went up in September, for example, the *Jewish Federation of Greater Los Angeles* site reads like a yellow pages, only faster and better, because the listings zero in on community organizations—food banks, loan associations, employment services, synagogues, schools.

The Greater Jewish center site can be reached through all browsers. Many others require either Microsoft's Internet Explorer or the Netscape Navigator.

Latino Net—in English only for now—falls short of its intended national scope. Employment and Events listings for Washington, D.C., and Puerto Rico are still under construction. Working links include News This Week (articles on Latino issues, including immigration, voting and business, broken down by state and region, and Education (scholarships and internships).

There are a multitude of Asian-American sites, some university-based, like the *Asian American Resources* page at the Massachusetts Institute of Technology, which organizes links to everything from lists of Asian-language videos, to clubs, to Asian-American media outlets and businesses. The *Asian American Network*, with several links to Taiwan-related sites, has information useful to entrepreneurs who often travel and work in both areas during the years-long immigration process.

Related Sites

Following are links to the external web sites mentioned in this article. These sites are not part of the *New York Times* on the Web, and the *Times* has no control over their content or availability. When you have finished visiting any of these sites, you will be able to return to this page by clicking on your web browser's "Back" button or icon until this page reappears.

Immigration and Naturalization Service
American Immigration Center
Immigration Lawyers on the Web
Asian American Network
Asian American Resources
Latino Net
Council of Jewish Federations
U.S. State Department
Jewish Federation of Greater Los Angeles

FURTHER REFERENCE

Castles, Stephen, and Mark J. Miller. *The Age of Migration: International Population Movements in the Modern World.* Guilford Press. 1998.

Danilov, Dam P., and Howard D. Deitsch. *Immmigrating to USA.* Self Counsel Press. 1998.

Flanders, Stephen A. *Atlas of American Migration.* Facts on File, Inc. 1998.

Garling, Scipio. *How to Win the Immigration Debate.* Federation for American Immigration Reform (FAIR). 1997.

Gyory, Andrew. *Closing the Gate: Race, Politics, and the Chinese Exclusion Act.* University of North Carolina Press. 1998.

Laguerre, Michael. *Diasporic Citizenship: Haitian Americans in Transnational America.* St. Martins Press. 1998.

Massey, Douglas. *Worlds in Motion: Understanding International Migration at the End of the Millenium.* Oxford University Press. 1998.

Papdemetriou, Demetrios G. *The Border and Beyond: Cooperation and Conflict on Migration Issues in U.S.-Mexico Relations.* Carnegie Endowment for International Peace. 1998.

Pickus, Noah, and Roger Smith, eds. *Immigration and Citizenship in the Twenty-First Century.* Rowman & Littlefield. 1998.

Reimers, David M. *Unwelcome Strangers: American Identity and the Turn against Immigration.* Columbia University Press. 1998.

4

SCHOOL PRAYER

On October 7, 1801, members of the Danbury Baptist Association, having been persecuted for lack of adherence to Congregationalism, the established religion of Connecticut, wrote a letter to newly elected President of the United States Thomas Jefferson. Declaring "That no man ought to suffer in name, person, or effects on account of his religious Opinions," the Baptists expressed their hope that Jefferson would exert his influence in the cause of religious freedom. In his reply to the Baptists on New Years Day, 1802, Jefferson announced his interpretation of the first amendment to the Constitution, stating the following in part:

> Believing with you that religion is a matter which lies solely between man and his God; that he owes account to none other for his faith or his worship; that the legislative powers of the government reach actions only, and not opinions, I contemplate with sovereign reverence that act of the whole American people which declared that their legislature should 'make no law respecting an establishment of religion, or prohibiting the free exercise thereof,' thus building a wall of separation between church and State.

Jefferson knew, as did the Danbury Baptists, that the predominant interpretation of the First Amendment in their day held that its wording was specifically formulated to preclude an official *national* religion, but not religions officially established by the states. The author of the amendment, James Madison, selected each and every word as a matter of political compromise: "Congress shall make no law respecting an establishment of religion." This wording, as Madison understood it, allowed Congress to neither establish a national church, nor to forbid the states, several of which had official churches, from doing so.

Many people at the time, including Madison and Jefferson, hoped that states would abolish their own official religions, and in the first half of the nineteenth century all of them did so. The disestablishment of state churches did not, however, end America's church-state controversy. Jefferson's response to the Danbury Baptists was one round in the church-state controversy that has periodically erupted in this country since 1620, when the Pilgrims landed at Plymouth Rock. Writing the Mayflower Compact as a social contract upon which the Pilgrims could build a civil government, William Bradford explained both why the Pilgrims had come to the New World, and the purpose for establishing a new society therein:

> Haveing undertaken, for ye glorie of God, and advancemente of ye Christian faith, and honour of our king & countrie, a voyage to plant ye first colonie in ye Northerne parts of Virginia, doe by these presents solemnly & mutualy in ye presence of God, and one of another, covenant & combine our selves togeather into a civill body politick, for our better ordering & preservation & furtherance of ye ends aforesaid;

Bradford and his comrades understood that they had come to practice the Christian faith as they understood it. They feared doctrinal accretions like those that had infected the Anglican and Roman Catholic Churches would plague them also, and so both they and their neighbors, the Puritans of the Massachusetts Bay Colony, banished religious dissenters from their company. The most famous dissident to part company with the Puritans was Roger Williams, who founded Providence, Rhode Island as asylum for people of all religious beliefs.

Over the course of the ensuing three and one half centuries, the church-state conflict in America has centered primarily on two issues. The first is state aid to religion in the form of either direct assistance to religious schools, or indirectly by provision of tax exemptions to nonprofit institutions. The second issue, examined in the following articles, is affirmation of religious belief in schools and other public institutions. This debate centers on two potentially conflictual phrases in the first amendment: "Congress shall make no law respecting an establishment of religion, or prohibiting the free exercise thereof." Some people claim that prayer in public schools is constitutionally protected as the free exercise of religion, while others see it as state establishment of religion.

Congress occasionally becomes engaged in the school prayer debate, as it did on May 7, 1998, when Oklahoma's Representative Earnest Istook introduced a constitutional amendment that stated the following:

> To secure the people's right to acknowledge God according to the dictates of conscience: The people's right to pray and to recognize their

religious beliefs, heritage, or traditions on public property, including schools, shall not be infringed. The Government shall not require any person to join in prayer or other religious activity, initiate or designate school prayers, discriminate against religion, or deny equal access to a benefit on account of religion.

The House voted against Istook's proposal by a vote of 224 to 203. Considering the narrowness of the issue's defeat it is likely that the issue will surface in Congress again, especially if conservatives acquire more seats in year 2000 elections. Most of the public battle over school prayer, however, has been waged in state legislatures and federal courts. The most prominent case in this controversy came to the U.S. Supreme court in 1962 under the name *Engel v. Vitale*. The New York State Board of Regents had recommended that public school children should recite together the following prayer at the beginning of each school day: "Almighty God, we acknowledge our dependence upon Thee, and we beg thy blessings upon us, our parents, our teachers, and our country." Engel and members of several religious liberties organizations challenged the prayer as an unconstitutional establishment of religion, stating that it is an obvious affirmation of belief in God, and also obviously sponsored by the state. Vitale and representatives of sixteen other states argued that the first amendment does not imply that government should be hostile to religion, and that recitation of the prayer is purely voluntary.

In his decision in this case, Justice Black invoked Jefferson's "wall of separation" metaphor:

> We think that by using its public school system to encourage recitation of the Regents' prayer, the State of New York has adopted a practice wholly inconsistent with the Establishment Clause. There can, of course, be no doubt that New York's program of daily classroom invocation of God's blessings as prescribed in the Regents' prayer is a religious activity. It is a solemn avowal of divine faith and supplication for the blessings of the Almighty.... The petitioners contend among other things that the state laws requiring or permitting use of the Regents' prayer must be struck down as a violation of the Establishment Clause because that prayer was composed by governmental officials as a part of a governmental program to further religious beliefs. For this reason, petitioners argue, the State's use of the Regents' prayer in its public school system breaches the constitutional wall of separation between Church and State. We agree with that contention since we think that the constitutional prohibition against laws respecting an establishment of religion must at least mean that in this country it is no part of the business of government to compose official prayers for any group of the American people to recite as a part of a religious program carried on by government.... The First Amendment was added to the Constitution to stand as a guarantee that neither the power nor the prestige of the Federal Government would be used to control, support or influence the kinds of

prayer the American people can say—that the people's religions must not be subjected to the pressures of government for change each time a new political administration is elected to office. Under that Amendment's prohibition against governmental establishment of religion, as reinforced by the provisions of the Fourteenth Amendment, government in this country, be it state or federal, is without power to prescribe by law any particular form of prayer which is to be used as an official prayer in carrying on any program of governmentally sponsored religious activity.

Following the *Engel* decision, school prayer advocates attempted a number of other measures, but they were also unsuccessful. An Alabama law, for example, provided for a moment of silence "for mediation or voluntary prayer," but in *Wallace v. Jaffree* (1985) the Supreme Court declared the law unconstitutional because the intent of its sponsors in the state legislature was to return prayer to public schools.

The following *New York Times* articles (on pages 67–83) explain the fate of Representative Istook's amendment, and then describe some other situations in which the school prayer issue has recently surfaced in politics.

The New York Times

Friday, June 5, 1998

House Rejects Drive to Allow Formal Prayer in the Schools

BY KATHARINE Q. SEELYE

For the first time in more than a quarter of a century, the House today debated—and rejected—an effort by religious conservatives to amend the Constitution to allow organized prayer in public schools.

The vote was 224 to 203 for the bill, a majority but 61 votes short of the two-thirds necessary to pass a constitutional amendment. The vote doomed the measure for now, but it had no future anyway in the Senate, where the right has less influence.

Students may already pray, read the Bible and engage in religious speech at school as long as they do so in a reasonable time, place and manner, without disrupting other students.

In addition to allowing organized prayer in school, the measure would have allowed religious symbols on public property, like a creche at a courthouse. It also would have allowed use of tax money for religious activities.

The measure drew the active opposition of religious groups from across the denominational spectrum, including Catholics, Jews, Presbyterians, Seventh-day Adventists and Muslims. They said the measure was unnecessary, would coerce religious minorities into conforming with the majority and would upend nearly 300 years of religious freedom guaranteed by the First Amendment.

"This amendment strips the individual of his or her rights to pick his or her own prayer or to practice his or her own religion without having to subject their beliefs to the manipulation and interference of an arrogant majority," said Representative Bobby Scott, Democrat of Virginia.

67

The size of the defeat was a blow to the religious right, which had intensified lobbying for the measure in recent days. Still the appearance of a school prayer measure on the floor for the first time since 1971 showed how eager Republican leaders were to accommodate the right. And conservatives claimed success in just having the matter brought to a vote and in winning a majority.

"We worked very hard," said Randy Tate, executive director of the Christian Coalition. "We want a seat at the table, and some would love to keep us out. We've always believed our influence should be commensurate with our numbers."

But others said the measure would hurt Republicans by showing the degree to which the right was influencing the fractured party, especially over such a divisive issue.

Laura W. Murphy, director of the Washington office of the American Civil Liberties Union, dismissed the measure as "something to galvanize the far-right constituencies because they are anticipating a close election in the fall."

"More denominations have been engaged in this battle," Ms. Murphy added, "and they've decided the Christian Coalition doesn't speak for them."

Conservatives argued that the amendment was needed to protect students from overly sensitive school administrators and misguided judges who twisted the idea of separation of church and state into a hostility toward religious expression.

"Basic liberties are being infringed because of judicial wrongheadedness and, frankly, secularist bias," Representative Henry Hyde, Republican of Illinois, said on the floor. "Neutrality towards religion, not hostility, is the ideal we seek."

Supporters also argued that the perceived hostility toward religious expression coincided with an increase in violence, crime and moral turpitude.

"As prayer has gone out of schools, guns, knives, drugs and gangs have come in," said Representative Ernest Istook Jr., the Oklahoma Republican who sponsored the measure. "It's time we put the emphasis on what we believe, and almost every American believes in God."

The amendment did not force anyone to pray, Mr. Istook said, but added that those who did not want to should not have the power to censor those who did.

"You don't have the right to shut people up and censor them just because you choose to be thin-skinned and intolerant when someone else is trying to express their faith," he said in the daylong debate.

Supporters and opponents argued that they were trying to protect the guarantees of freedom of religion on which the nation was founded.

This only annoyed lawmakers like Representative Amo Houghton of

New York, one of 28 Republicans who voted against the measure. A total of 197 Republicans and 27 Democrats favored it.

"Both sides claim to be on the side of the righteous," Mr. Houghton said on the House floor, but he suggested that the sponsors seemed to have conflicting motives.

"People are screaming about getting the Government off our backs," he said, "but they turn around and have the Government tell our children how to pray."

The New York Times

June 28, 1998

Church, State, and School:
Holes in the Wall of Separation

BY ETHAN BRONNER

After a substitute teacher in a New York City public school led 11-year-old pupils in prayer and asked them to accept Jesus Christ as their savior, the Board of Education dismissed her this month. In the words of the board's spokeswoman, the teacher "had very clearly crossed the line."

Who could argue? If the separation of church and state mandated by the First Amendment means anything, surely it bars state-paid teachers from evangelizing to public schoolchildren in state-provided classrooms during school hours.

Yet the fired teacher, Mildred Rosario, has become a minor hero to some. Parents, New York Mayor Rudolph Giuliani and even the Republican congressional leadership have complained that, at a time when public schools are littered with needles and condoms, to fire a teacher for leading prayers is incomprehensible.

The episode is an apt reminder that 36 years after the Supreme Court banned school prayer, there is no consensus on the appropriate links between government and religion, particularly within the school system.

Two days after Ms. Rosario's prayer, another storm over church, state and schoolhouse erupted after a decision by the Wisconsin Supreme Court. It ruled that Milwaukee could spend taxpayer money to send pupils to religious schools through a voucher system.

Civil liberties advocates and teacher unions expressed shock that the court would permit state financing of institutions devoted to religious teaching.

But government aid to religious instruction has existed throughout U.S. history. Through most of the 19th century, public schools routinely taught the Bible. And even in this century, when the wall of separation became commonly invoked, religious schools have received substantial state subsidies.

Since 1947, when the Supreme Court permitted New Jersey to reimburse parochial school parents for the use of public school buses, large amounts of government money have gone to church-sponsored institutions. Not only are church properties tax-exempt—no small matter in places like Manhattan—but parochial school parents in some states get tax breaks for tuition, and the equivalent of public vouchers are widely used in church preschools and colleges. Churches and their schools have, of course, always benefitted from state-financed police and fire protection.

The devil has been in the details.

Parochial schools may use state-provided buses for transportation to classes but not for field trips; state-paid nurses may work at the schools but state-paid guidance counselors may not; the state may lend parochial schools textbooks but not audio-visual aids or maps (a distinction that led Sen. Daniel Patrick Moynihan, D-N.Y., to quip that the next big challenge would be atlases, which are books of maps). For years, public remedial teachers could serve parochial students only in trailers, a decision that the High Court reversed last year, thereby permitting the state teachers to enter the schools.

Religious display rulings have been even more tortured. A city may erect a creche at Christmas or a menorah at Hanukkah on condition that it is surrounded by enough other seasonal symbols, like reindeer or plastic candy canes, to blunt its religious message.

As bizarre as some of these distinctions may sound, they emerged from numerous cases over half a century. Most rulings came from divided courts and each established a slightly different set of criteria for interpreting the First Amendment's command that "Congress shall make no law respecting an establishment of religion, or prohibiting the free exercise thereof."

Given the founders' history—they were running from regimes that imposed religion—it is no accident that religious freedom leads the list of rights Congress is forbidden to abridge, or that on its heels come speech and assembly. But the three form a nexus of individual liberty that is exceedingly difficult to disentangle. Shifting criteria reflect shifting legal and political climates as well as shifting Supreme Court personnel.

For example, it was Justice Hugo Black who wrote the 5–4 opinion in 1947 permitting New Jersey to reimburse parents for sending their children to parochial schools on public transportation. He said the First Amendment "requires the state to be neutral in its relations with groups of religious believers and nonbelievers." He added: "It does not require the state to be their adversary. State power is no more to be used so as to handicap religions, than it is to favor them."

Twenty years later, in a case from New York state, Justice Byron White wrote a 6–3 decision permitting the state to lend textbooks to parochial schools, saying the books were secular and would not be used for religious instruction. But Black, whose broad interpretation of the First Amendment had helped White craft that decision, dissented, saying there was a distinction between aid for things like transportation and lunch, which were non-substantive, and textbooks, which could be related to religious views.

And even though textbook loans were permitted, a decision in the 1970s barred the lending of instructional materials, including maps, to parochial schools "because of the predominantly religious character of the schools."

In 1985, the court barred public school teachers from performing remedial work in parochial schools. Among the dissenters was Associate Justice William H. Rehnquist, the future chief justice, who was instrumental in the 1997 ruling overturning that decision.

The back-and-forth on these questions suggests that if the Wisconsin voucher decision is accepted for review by the Supreme Court, something both sides say they want, the chances of a clear ruling seem small. Four other states have similar cases pending and voucher systems are rapidly spreading across the country.

Apart from the fear that such programs would denude the public schools of motivated pupils and much-needed cash, the concern of those opposed to the voucher program has been that if government is seen to endorse one religion, that religion has an unfair advantage over others.

The founders actually banned government endorsement largely for a different reason. They feared state involvement would sully religion, not help it.

Black relied on that view when he wrote that the First Amendment "rested on the belief that a union of government and religion tends to destroy government and to degrade religion." He added that the history of established religion "showed that many people lost their respect for any religion that had relied upon the support of government to spread its faith."

Advocates for a lowered wall of separation invoke the founders frequently, saying they never planned for government to be a force for atheism. That is true, but the founders insisted on religious freedom, mindful of something else: the danger of sectarian battle.

It is true that there appears little risk of a return to the religious wars of an earlier era. But a contemporary version—a battle between religious and secular forces for control of public and educational life—does not seem out of the question.

The New York Times

May 19, 1998

Alabama Governor's Obsession with School Prayer Issue Creating Schism in G.O.P.

By KEVIN SACK

TUSCALOOSA, ALA.—Even his campaign advisers are telling Gov. Fob James Jr. of Alabama to change the subject. But when it comes to his obsessive crusade to reconcile church and state, the governor has maintained the relentless tenacity he once showed as a hunkered-down halfback for the Auburn University Tigers.

His defiant stands in defense of religious expression in schools and courtrooms, including threats to call out the National Guard and defy the U.S. Supreme Court, have earned the governor a national reputation for zealotry—and some serious opposition in the Republican gubernatorial primary on June 2.

The campaign has already exposed deep fault lines here in the heart of the Republican South, a conflicted region that is at once stridently conservative and increasingly sensitive about its image. On one side are many of the Christian conservatives who have supplied the party with much of its energy and voting strength in recent years. On the other are many in the state's image-conscious business community, who fear that James is driving away investment.

Ralph Reed, the former director of the Christian Coalition and a consultant for James, said that the race is no longer merely about personalities or candidates.

"It's become a race about a set of issues that if rejected in a Republican primary will be a major setback to the pro-family movement across America," Reed said. "I think the pro-faith community is sophisticated enough to understand that."

James' opponents, who share his support for returning prayer to the public schools, counter that the race is not about beliefs. Instead, they say, it is about tactics, and whether the state can afford another governor known primarily for tilting at the federal courts.

Although James, 63, is favored in the five-man race, many political analysts assume that he will fail to win a majority in the primary and will be forced into a runoff on June 30. His most likely opponent is Winton Blount 3d, 54, a wealthy Montgomery businessman and party leader who accused James of "playing to the worst instincts" of this notoriously populist state.

In the 1960s, one of James' predecessors, George Wallace, achieved legendary status in Alabama with his populist, court-bashing defense of segregation. Now, more than 30 years later, James has adopted a similar approach, with religion replacing race as the focus of his appeal.

Unlike Wallace, whose racist rants were at least partly manufactured for political effect, James' stands on religion seem to be heartfelt, according to those who know him best. But he also has chosen to advertise his views during the campaign with stump speeches and legal briefs, making school prayer as prominent a feature of his re-election strategy as are his pledges to improve schools and hold down taxes.

In an effort to energize evangelicals, the single largest component of the Republican electorate in Alabama, some of James' strategists have portrayed the race as a referendum on a distinct brand of social conservatism.

But James' aides also recognize that the campaign has revealed fissures within the conservative Christian movement between those who admire James' resolve and those who fear that his showmanship may undermine their cause. They have kept the prayer issue out of his television advertisements, preferring instead to target their appeals to evangelicals through telephone calls and direct mail. And they have encouraged James to focus his remarks more on education, taxes, jobs and crime.

"Prayer is a strong issue and it reinforces Fob James' strong base," said Emory Folmar, the mayor of Montgomery and James' campaign chairman. "But I think everybody has established positions on it and he would be better served to move on to these other things."

James showed no signs of doing that this week. While addressing some 70 supporters at a Piccadilly cafeteria here—a campaign luncheon that began with a prayer "in Jesus' name"—the governor raised the issue of prayer in the schools not once, but twice.

"The First Amendment of the U.S. Constitution says Congress shall make no law respecting the establishment of religion or prohibiting the free exercise thereof," James said, backed by placards exclaiming "More Fob!" "A high school football coach and 30 or 40 youngsters saying the Lord's Prayer before kickoff does not establish a national church in the United States of America. And when a judge tells you that, that judge is wrong and that judge needs to be corrected."

During the last 15 months, James has waged a relentless guerrilla war against the courts over long-held interpretations of the First Amendment's establishment clause. The U.S. Supreme Court has ruled consistently in school prayer cases that the clause prohibits government from favoring religion over non-religion. James has charged that the courts have far exceeded their authority, misread the Constitution, and suppressed religious freedom.

In February 1997, he announced that he would call out the National Guard if necessary to defend the right of Judge Roy Moore of Etowah County Circuit Court to display the Ten Commandments in his courtroom. Another state court judge ruled that Moore must remove the wooden tablet, but the decision was overturned by the state Supreme Court on technical grounds.

Last June, James wrote a 34-page letter to Judge Ira DeMent of federal district court urging him to dismiss a challenge to a 1993 Alabama statute that permitted non-sectarian, non-proselytizing, student-initiated voluntary prayer in public schools. The letter essentially argued that the Bill of Rights does not apply to the states. "We will have no justice in our courts or integrity in our government without the blessing of God upon us," James wrote.

DeMent rejected the governor's request, and later ruled that the school prayer statute was unconstitutional. When the judge issued an injunction last November explaining what forms of religious expression were allowed and proscribed in the schools (prayers at sporting events were prohibited), James vowed to "resist Judge DeMent's order by every legal and political means with every ounce of strength I possess."

This month, James petitioned the U.S. Supreme Court to overturn DeMent's ruling, with a brief that encouraged defiance of the high court. "In the absence of constitutional limitations, other constitutional officials throughout government owe no 'deference' to the decisions of this Court," James argued in the brief, which was written by his son, Forrest H. James III. He added: "It is undoubtedly true that the people of this country have the constitutional right, if they so choose, to march forthrightly into hell; but they should not be taken there, blindfolded and against their will, by the U.S. Supreme Court."

The Alabama attorney general, Bill Pryor, a Republican, quickly distanced himself from James, saying that the governor did not speak for the state. Pryor, who was appointed by James last year to fill an unexpired term, has filed a separate appeal with the 11th U.S. Circuit Court of Appeals. That appeal accepts the unconstitutionality of school prayer, but uses free speech grounds to challenge some of DeMent's restrictions.

In addition to Blount, who finished third in the 1994 Republican primary, James' other opponents in this year's primary are former Gov. Guy Hunt, 64, who was pardoned recently on a state ethics conviction and is running to recapture the office he was forced to resign in 1993; Lewis Leslie

McAllister Jr., 65, a Tuscaloosa manufacturer and local party leader, and Phillip Williams, 58, a former state finance director under James.

The most recent public poll, which was conducted April 27–30 for Southern Opinion Research, showed Blount (pronounced blunt) moving into contention with James. Among those who said they were likely to vote in the Republican primary, James was supported by about 39 percent, Blount by 30 percent, Hunt by 14 percent, McAllister by 9 percent and Williams by 2 percent. Seven percent said they were undecided, and the margin of error was plus or minus 5 percentage points.

The Republican nominee, presumably with a depleted treasury, will likely face Lt. Gov. Don Siegelman, a Democrat, in the general election. Siegelman is a telegenic and experienced candidate who had raised $3.9 million as of April 15. With little competition in the primary, he has managed to save nearly all of it.

Support for James, who made a fortune manufacturing plastic-coated barbells before beginning his political career, is particularly anemic in Alabama's business community. Those white-collar Republicans form the core of Blount's base. They blame James for failing to win legislative support for tort reform, for exacerbating the perception of the state as a backwater, and for devoting more energy to religious issues than to economic development.

The governor won a big victory last fall by bringing a Boeing rocket booster plant and 3,000 jobs to Decatur, Ala., with more than $140 million in state incentives. But it may have come too late to restore his reputation in business circles.

Blount, whose father served as postmaster general in the Nixon Administration, said the state "is thirsting for leadership, thirsting to join the other states marching proudly into the 21st century." And while he emphasized that he, too, supports prayer in the schools, he said he would respect the rule of law and would not be "out running ragged on some strategy that doesn't make any sense."

After beginning their television advertising campaign, James' aides maintained that they have stopped Blount's momentum. But Blount has received endorsements in recent weeks from the leading newspapers in the state's four largest cities. And he has won the endorsement of the Coalition of Christians for Family Values, a group of evangelicals led by a Montgomery minister, Mickey A. Kirkland, who ran in the Republican primary in 1994.

Kirkland said that James has alienated many conservative Christians by turning the school prayer debate into a sideshow.

"I think people of faith see the sensationalizing of issues for political gain, and we despise that, detest that," Kirkland said.

He said that James also lost support last month when a television station's microphone captured him cursing while signing a bill requiring a moment of silent reflection at the start of each school day. The governor later apologized, but Kirkland said that some evangelicals saw hypocrisy.

Other conservative Christian groups are firmly on James' side, and Reed is confident that a heavy turnout of evangelicals will insure victory for the governor. Robert Russell, chairman of the Christian Coalition of Alabama, which does not endorse candidates, predicted that James would win "tremendous support from the Christian right" because of his support for prayer in the schools and the Ten Commandments and his opposition to abortion.

The New York Times

July 1, 1998

Alabama Governor Wins Runoff in Triumph for the Right

By Kevin Sack

MONTGOMERY, ALA.—In a convincing victory for religious conservatives, Gov. Fob James Jr. won a decisive majority tonight over the businessman Winton Blount 3d in Alabama's Republican primary runoff for governor.

The Governor's triumph sets up another intriguing battle, in the general election in November, when James will face Lieut. Gov. Don Siegelman, who easily won the Democratic nomination four weeks ago. Siegelman, who has hoarded cash while the Republicans skirmished, hopes that his proposal for a new lottery to finance education will help break the Republicans' near stranglehold on statewide offices in this once solidly Democratic state.

The caustic Republican campaign was seen very much as a referendum on James, 63, whose unvarnished political style and strong support for school prayer have made him a modern-day emblem of Southern defiance. In his campaign, the Governor alternated between Christian professions of God-fearing faith and a less charitable take on his opponent, whom he mocked for his heft and his inherited wealth.

The race also provided an unobstructed view of the strains facing the South's newly dominant Republican Party. While each man embraced some of the other's positions, James spoke most passionately to the state's social conservatives while Blount harped on the need to accelerate economic growth.

With 93 percent of precincts reporting, James led Blount by 56 percent to 44 percent. The Governor finished first in the five-man primary on June 2, but could not [win] enough to escape a runoff.

"It's always good to have a tough scrimmage or two before the big game," said a beaming James after declaring victory tonight. "And I've had two."

For the adaptable James, an Auburn University football star who made a fortune selling plastic-coated barbells, today's victory extends a resilient political career. James has switched parties twice in the last two decades, and he has needed a runoff to win his party's nomination in each of three campaigns for governor. He first renounced his Republican roots before running successfully for governor as a Democrat in 1978. After choosing not to seek a second term, he switched back to the Republican Party to run in 1994.

A poll taken last week showed this year's race to be a dead heat, with Blount leading by a single percentage point. But in the end, the mechanics of a midsummer runoff with few other races on the ballot favored James, who apparently succeeded in pulling his Christian conservative supporters to the polls. Last week's survey, which was taken for three Alabama newspapers, showed that he was overwhelmingly favored by those who said they took the Bible to be literal truth.

James and his advisers did not shy from his identification with the religious right. In advertisements and public appearances, James boasted about his quixotic efforts to reverse the U.S. Supreme Court's three-decade-old rulings against school prayer.

James's lead consultant, Ralph Reed, the former executive director of the Christian Coalition, contended that the election would serve as a national test of the strength of Christian conservatives. "I don't need to tell you that in God's wisdom and planning, the eyes of America are going to be on Alabama on June 30," Reed told a group of ministers last week.

Blount took pains to insist that he, too, was for returning prayer to the schools. But he argued that James's open talk of sedition, including a court brief suggesting that Supreme Court rulings do not bind the states, had been a national embarrassment. In addition to distracting attention from the need to improve schools and recruit new industry, Blount said, the Governor's approach to school prayer harked back to the days when Gov. George C. Wallace used state's rights arguments to stymie desegregation.

Blount, 54, is the son of Winton M. Blount, a Montgomery construction and manufacturing magnate. The younger Blount owns automobile dealerships and a plastics company, and he outspent James by nearly two to one, financing his campaign with his own money and that of his family. The centerpiece of his campaign was a proposal to eliminate the state's 4 percent sales tax on food, which served to counter James's pledge not to raise state taxes.

Blount had hoped to benefit from an unusual provision that allows all Alabama voters to participate in a Republican primary runoff, regardless of whether they voted or how they voted in the first primary. Last week,

Mayor Richard Arrington Jr. of Birmingham, a five-term Democrat, endorsed Blount for the Republican nomination and announced that his mostly black political machine, the Jefferson County Citizens Coalition, would work to turn out Democratic votes for him.

James's strategists worried that Democratic voters could provide the margin of victory for Blount. But they worked assiduously in the campaign's final days to encourage a backlash by portraying Arrington as a liberal Democratic boss who had demanded concessions on appointments and spending priorities from Blount. That contention was denied by both men.

In a final television advertisement broadcast last weekend, James charged that "Winton Blount sold out the Republican Party." Picturing Blount beside Arrington, who is black, the advertisement asked, "If he wins Tuesday, who'll be the real Governor?" Mr Blount accused James of making a racial appeal, an accusation he denied.

[Editor's note: In the November general election, Fob James was defeated by Democrat Donald Siegelman, who received 58 percent of the vote compared to James's 42 percent.]

Questions for Class Discussion or Debate

As you conduct further research on school prayer or church-state relations, many questions may come to your mind. If you plan to debate these issues in class, you may want to consider arguing positions related to the following statements:

- God intended America to be a Christian nation.
- Nondenominational voluntary prayer in public schools is potentially harmful.
- Nondenominational voluntary prayer in public schools is a violation of the establishment clause of the First Amendment.
- Disallowing nondenominational voluntary prayer school is a violation of the freedom of religion clause of the First Amendment.

Resources for Class Debates and Further Study

School Prayer on the Internet

This Library of Congress web site contains many resources concerning the history of church-state relations in the United States.
http://lcweb.loc.gov/exhibits/religion/

The Freedom Forum Online, Religion Page
http://www.freedomforum.org/religion/welcome.asp#schools

The American Civil Liberties Union
http://www.aclu.org/issues/religion/hmrf.html

Christian Legal Society
http://www.clsnet.com/welcome.html

People for the American Way
http://www.pfaw.org/

The Rutherford Institute
http://www.rutherford.org/

Further Reference

Alley, Robert S. *School Prayer: The Court, the Congress, and the First Amendment.* Prometheus Books. 1994.

Andryszewski, Tricia. *School Prayer: A History of the Debate* (Issues in Focus Series). Enslow Publishers, Inc. 1997.

Fenwick, Lynda Beck. *Should the Children Pray?: A Historical, Judicial, and Political Examination of Public School Prayer.* Baylor University Press. 1998.

5

BILINGUAL EDUCATION

What is the significance of language? The following lines are presented as a demonstration of the importance of language:

Εαν ταις γλωσσαις των ανθρωπων λαλω και των αγγελων, αγαπην δε μη εχω, γεγονα χαλκος ηχων η κυμβαλον αλαλαζον. και εαν εχω προφητειαν και ειδω τα μυστηρια παντα και πασαν την γνωσιν, και εαν εχω πασαν την πιστιν ωστε ορη μεθισταναι, αγαπην δε μη εχω, ουθεν ειμι. καν ψωμισω παντα τα υπαρχοντα μου, και εαν παραδω το σωμα μου ινα καυχησωμαι, αγαπην δε μη εχω, ουδεν ωφελουμαι.... νυνι δε μενει πιστις, ελπις, αγαπη, τα τρια ταυτα: μειζων δε τουτων η αγαπη.

Having trouble reading the above paragraph? If it seems "Greek to you," you are right—Greek it is. If you do not read Greek, these lines are unintelligible, but if you do read Greek, not only can you decipher their meaning, but the full richness of the nuances of the original language is also available to you. If you do not read Greek, you have only the impoverished version that even a good English translation provides:

If I speak in the tongues of men and of angels, but have not love, I am only a resounding gong or a clanging cymbal. If I have the gift of prophecy and can fathom all mysteries and all knowledge, and if I have a faith that can move mountains, but have not love, I am nothing. If I give all I possess to the poor and surrender my body to the flames, but have not love, I gain nothing. Love is patient, love is kind. It does not envy, it does not boast, it is not proud.... And now these three remain: faith, hope and love. But the greatest of these is love. (NIV 1 Cor. 13: 1–4, 13).

Interestingly enough, some scholars believe these words (at the bottom of the previous page) may have originally been written in Aramaic or Hebrew, and so the English translation may be two languages removed from the original.

The depth of nuance, tradition, and meaning in any language is at least partly lost in translation. Although we may speak a foreign language with exceptional facility, we are never more than imposters when that language is the mother tongue. We cannot conceive its richness.

Now let us suppose that we are Americans who move from Vermont to Greece. In order to participate fully in the culture that surrounds us, we must learn to read and write Greek. Perhaps we would expect to do so. Perhaps also, however, we would encounter some unexpected problems. In Greek schools our children are learning to read, write, and speak in Greek. Although Greece is a venerable and ancient culture, we find our children thinking more and more like Greeks and losing their American heritage. After several years of this progress, in some quite important but hard to describe ways, our children start to become strangers to us. We want them to know Greek, but we also want them to know American English, and to remain true descendants of the rich American culture from which they have come. We know that if they are not fluent in English, they will not read in their full richness *The Great Gatsby, Moby Dick*, or even a novel by Stephen King. As parents of children who are losing a culture we love, we consider asking the local schools to provide classes in which our children can learn in English as well as Greek. The local Greeks are offended. They tell us that if we live in their country we should speak their language and adopt their culture. We are dismayed.

Thousands of Mexican, Japanese, and other families face this problem in American neighborhoods every day. Feelings run deep on both sides of the issue. In order to understand these feelings we must further understand two things. The first is the power of language. If we take French or Spanish in high school, we may get the mistaken impression that learning a second language is no big deal, that language itself means little. Only when we encounter the power of language and its force in the lives of others do we understand the depth of feeling that language creates.

To more accurately perceive the power of language that underlies the bilingual education debate, we take a momentary detour to read two articles: The article on pages 89–93 by John Edgar Wideman, the author of "Brothers and Keepers," illustrates the potential power of language in our lives. Language, as Wideman illustrates in his well-crafted essay, is essential to our personal identities. We may ask, however, is there not still value in learning another language? A strong affirmation of the value of learning another language may be found in the article by Mireya Navarro on pages 95–97.

𝕿𝖍𝖊 𝕹𝖊𝖜 𝖄𝖔𝖗𝖐 𝕿𝖎𝖒𝖊𝖘

January 13, 1985

The Language of Home

BY JOHN EDGAR WIDEMAN

Why do writers write about the same place over and over again? There are probably as many answers to this question as there are writers obsessed with a city, a country, a village or a community. Rather than try to speak for others whose one certified virtue is speaking well for themselves, I'll focus my thoughts on the turn my own work has taken, my excursions home again, home again in fiction and nonfiction, to Homewood, a black neighborhood in Pittsburgh.

In the green woods of Maine, beside a lake, 2,200 miles from my present home in Wyoming, even farther in most ways from the cityscapes of my imagination, there is a gray wooden lawn chair perched on the edge of a dock. The setting is crucial. Like most writers, I observe rituals. A meticulously arranged scenario, certain pens, paper, a time of day, an alignment of furniture, particular clothing, coffee cooled to a precise temperature—the variations are infinite, but each writer knows his or her version of the preparatory ritual must be exactly duplicated if writing is to begin, prosper.

Repetition dignifies these rituals. My return home begins with a ceremony. Early morning is my time. Bundled in a hooded sweatsuit, more a protection against mosquitoes than weather, I slouch in my gray chair at the end of the dock facing Long Lake. The morning play of water, wind and light has never been the same once in the 18 summers I've watched. From where I sit, it's almost two miles to the opposite shore. Picture a long, dark, ominous spine, low-hanging mist, white birches leaning over the water, a stillness so profound you can hear fish breaking the surface to catch insects. Whatever kind of weather they happen to be producing, the elements are always perfectly harmonized, synchronized.

The trick is to borrow, to internalize for a few quiet instants, the peace of the elements at play. Whatever mood or scene I'm attempting to capture, the first condition is inner calm, a simultaneous grasping and letting go that allows me to be a witness, a mirror. This state has gradually become more accessible to me only after fighting for years to believe again in my primal perceptions, my primal language, the words, gestures and feelings of my earliest memories. At some point I taught myself to stop translating from one language to another. I've learned I can say the things I want to say using the words and telling the stories of Homewood people. The blackness of my writing inheres in its history, its bilingual, Creole, maroon, bastardized, miscegenated, cross-cultural acceptance of itself in the mirror only it can manufacture.

I was once a paperboy. To deliver *The Pittsburgh Post-Gazette*, I had to climb Negley Avenue Hill. On bad days, with a sack of newspapers slung over my back, the cobbled hill seemed almost vertical, and I mounted it hand over hand with the help of an invisible rope anchored at the crest. Because rich white people resided at the top of Negley, the climb was almost worthwhile. They tipped royally, compensating me for the rigors of the ascent, the enormous distances separating their houses. I whistled a lot as I made my rounds. The turf atop Negley Hill remained foreign. Immense houses of stone and brick, long curving driveways, sculpted trees and shrubberies, lawns cleaner than most people's living-room floors. If I wasn't whistling, I was singing inside my head. The music of the Drifters, Dells, Turbans, Spaniels, Miracles, Flamingos, Louis Berry, Jerry Butler, all the quartets and stars in whose songs I could imagine a shape for my feelings.

On those lily-white streets bordering the Squirrel Hill section of Pittsburgh, I knew I was an intruder. Would I be discovered, punished? The songs were protection, a talisman, but they also could betray me. If anybody ever heard the music inside my head, I'd be in real trouble. Though I couldn't have articulated it at the time, I sensed that my music wove an alternate version of reality, one that included me and incriminated me, one that could sweep away the stones. Some evenings I was buoyed by the danger, the trespass I was committing, walking those sleepy streets, carrying doo-wop and "Oh What a Night" and "For Your Precious Love," contraband in my skull.

Thirty years later, and things haven't changed much. I return to Pittsburgh again and again in my writing. Three books of fiction, a nonfiction narrative, "Brothers and Keepers," a pair of new novels in the works, all rooted in Homewood, the actual black community where I was raised, the imaginary landscape I dream up as I go along. Every book a voyage home, each a struggle up a steep incline whose familiarity makes it more rather than less difficult. I find myself, each time a book is finished, in an alien place, whistling, singing to keep away the strangers who own the hilltop and everything else.

On our way back and forth to Peabody High School, my partner Scott Payne and I crossed Penn Avenue, the main drag of East Liberty, which was in those days a thriving pocket of stores, theaters, banks and restaurants. On Penn Avenue was a confectioner's we liked to ogle. One day as we stared at the windowload of fanciful sweets, I said to Scott in my best stuck-up, siddity white folks' voice, "The prices here are exorbitant," emphasizing the final exotic word, precisely chopping it into four syllables, the orotund "or" deep in my throat the way I'd heard somebody somewhere say it. A nicely dressed white lady who would have been quite at home on Negley Hill laying that extra 25 or 50 cents on me when I collected at the end of the week heard me say "exorbitant" and did a wide-eyed double take. If I'd yelled an obscenity at her, she couldn't have looked more shocked, outraged. She regarded her companion, another middle-aged, coifed-for-shopping matron, and the two of them wagged their heads in dismay.

Did you hear that? Did you hear what he said?...

Not until years later did I begin to guess at the nature of my offense. I'd stolen a piece of their language. Not only was it in my possession, I also had the nerve to flaunt it in a public place, in their righteous faces. To them a colored kid with a big word instead of a watermelon in his mouth wasn't even funny. I was peeking under their clothes, maybe even shouting that they, like the emperor, weren't wearing any.

Language is power. I was fighting skirmishes in a battle still engaging me—legitimizing the language of my tribe. The songs in my head on Negley Hill, the fancy word I appropriated and mocked surveying in a shop window sweets I couldn't afford were means I had developed to create sense in a world that insistently denied me. When my family moved to Shadyside so I could attend "better" schools and we were one of only three or four black families in the neighborhood, I learned to laugh with the white guys when we hid in a stairwell outside Liberty School gym and passed around a "nigarette." I hated it when a buddy took a greedy, wet puff, "nigger-lipping" a butt before he passed it on to me. Speaking out, identifying myself with the group being slurred by these expressions, was impossible. I had neither the words nor the heart. I talked the talk and walked the walk of the rest of my companions.

When Lavinia, my first love, on leave one summer from Harlem to visit her grandfather, who boarded in my grandparents' house, urged me to wear my jeans slung low on my hips like the black boys and Spanish boys she'd left behind on Convent Avenue, her distaste for the white kids' style, her assertion that another way was both possible and better, struck me with the force of revelation. At 13 Lavinia possessed a woman's body, and the fact that she would let me, only 13 myself, touch it kept me in a constant state of agitation and awe. She was larger than life and grew more fascinating, more like a goddess as she described Harlem's black ways, its authority to be what it wished to be. Lavinia didn't exactly hate whites; they were beneath her contempt. It dawned on me that there was a Negley Hill where my white buddies, those unconscious kings of the earth, would be scared to deliver papers.

I've taught Ralph Ellison's "Invisible Man" to many classes, lots of people, including Lois, a fundamentalist Christian from Wyoming who was so shocked by the language and situations dramatized in the books of my Afro-American literature class that she threatened to report me to my chairman unless I allowed her to skip the readings her husband, a one-man board of censors, found objectionable. There was also David Bradley, who sat through one of my first fumbling attempts to teach black writing at the University of Pennsylvania and went on to produce a prizewinning novel, "The Chaneysville Incident," which absorbed and extended the traditions Mr. Ellison affirms. I return to "Invisible Man" not because of a scarcity of good books by black authors but because without Mr. Ellison's work in the mix—monumental, prophetic, bristling with flashes of light—something necessary has been left unsaid, something's missing no matter what combination of books and authors I select for a course.

Mr. Ellison's vision is indispensable because it makes tangible so much of the fiber, the nuance, connecting other Afro-American writers to him and one another. "Invisible Man" is a home, and Afro-American writers predictably return to it. Although its faults—a protagonist whose abstractness inhibits a reader's emotional identification with him, episodes brilliant in themselves but too long, too allegorical, too distracting from the narrative sequence, minor, stereotypical roles for its female characters—cause the novel to be like any home, less than perfect, it also has the incalculable advantages of home cooking. For many of us, "Invisible Man" came first, educating our palates, defining what's good, stamping our tastes for a lifetime.

My wife, Judy, has spent almost every summer of her life in Maine. For her the lake and pinewoods of Camp Takajo are a special place. She's found no other spot on earth that duplicates the haunting dance of sunlight as it seeps down through the dark trunks of the pine trees. Because she taught me to see this indwelling spirit that animates the green woods, it lives now, not only in trees but in her. Certain affinities, constellations of meaning are triggered for me by arrangements and rearrangements of green, light and shadow. A green robe Judy wears, a path fringed with greenery winding from cabin to lake, feathery pine branches a hundred feet up that crackle with light when wind stirs them, all these images connect, permeate each other.

Words, objects, rituals have the power to shine forth. They accumulate this power, this endless string of associations presiding Januslike backward and forward in time, because by circumstance or choice we must return to them. We live many lives, and the confusion, the chaos of a splintered existence is lessened a bit by the riveting flashes that connect our multiple selves to one another and to other lives. When I write I want to show how simple acts, simple words can be transformed to release their spiritual force. This is less a conscious esthetic to be argued or analyzed than a determination to draw from the unique voices of Homewood's people the means for documenting the reality of their attitudes and emotions. I want to trace the comings and goings of my people on the invisible plane of existence where so much of the substance of black life resides.

Everyone lives a significant portion of life below the surface. Art records and elaborates this unseen dimension. A minority culture systematically prevented from outward expression of its dreams, wishes and aspirations must evolve ways for both individuals and the group to sustain its underground life. Afro-Americans have become experts at living in at least two places simultaneously, cultivating a sensitivity to the distance—comic, ironic, tragic—between our outer and inner lives. For us music, speech and body movement are repositories for preserving history, values, dignity, a sense of ourselves as separate, whole. Double-entendre, signifying, mimicry, call-and-response patterns of storytelling, oratory and song, style as cutting edge, as a weapon against enforced anonymity have been honed to display and protect our secrets.

One of the earliest lessons I learned as a child was that if you looked away from something, it might not be there when you looked back. I feared loss, feared turning to speak to someone and finding no one there. Being black and poor reinforced the wisdom of a tentative purchase on experience. Don't get too close, doubt what you think you see. Need, commitment set you up for a fall, create the conditions for disaster. If you let your eyes touch lightly, rely on an impressionistic touch and go, then you may achieve the emotional economy of faint gains, faint losses. Writing forces me to risk ignoring the logic of this lesson. Another legacy from Mr. Ellison, the implicit challenge he poses—who will write our history?—has helped turn me around. The stance, the habit of looking long and hard, especially at those things—a face, a hand, a home—that matter, makes them matter more and more. I examine minutely the place I come from, repeat its stories, sing its songs, preserve its language and values, because they make me what I am and because if I don't, who will?

The New York Times

September 8, 1998

Bilingual Author Finds
Something Gained in Translation

By Mireya Navarro

SAN JUAN, P.R.—Her mother died 30 years ago, but for most of those years Rosario Ferré, one of Puerto Rico's leading writers, found that event impossible to deal with in her work. It was only when she began to write in English, Ms. Ferré says, that she felt distant enough to explore in her fiction a subject that had been taboo in her native Spanish.

With English she discovered "a psychological distance," she said. "It's as if another person were writing."

Ms. Ferré, 59, is one of those rare writers who are successful in two languages. Her first novel in English, "The House on the Lagoon," was a National Book Award finalist in 1995. Her second, "Eccentric Neighborhoods," was published this year to critical praise. Both novels, published by Farrar, Straus & Giroux, render a historical portrait of 20th-century Puerto Rico through the fortunes of several families, mostly from the island's upper class.

Known as a feminist, satirist and literary critic, Ms. Ferré has a bachelor's degree in English literature from Manhattanville College and a master's and doctorate in Hispanic-American literature, from the University of Puerto Rico and the University of Maryland respectively. She had published more than a dozen books in Spanish, including novels, poems, essays, short stories and children's works before she started on "The House on the Lagoon" in 1991.

She began learning English at 7 in a Roman Catholic school in Puerto Rico and later honed her skill in the United States, where she taught college and lived for years. But she began to write in English purely for practical reasons, she said: to get better distribution for her work and thus reach a wider audience.

What she did not bargain for, she said, was the change in the creative process as she wrote, and often struggled, with her second language. In Spanish, words came to her so quickly and in such abundance that she could forget her point. English slowed her down, forcing her to consult dictionaries and thesauruses to expand vocabulary and giving her more time to figure out what her characters would do next. She found she could concentrate better on the story line and structure the plot more efficiently.

"When I get into Spanish, I go crazy with words," she said in an interview. "In English, I don't have the same linguistic repertory. I have no choice but to wear blinders and go straight."

Ms. Ferré calls her Spanish prose baroque, its elaborate style full of adjectives and complex syntax. In English, a more concise language, her novels are 35 to 50 pages shorter. She has acquired both brevity and a different sensibility.

"You go at different speeds," she said, comparing languages to trains. "You stop at different stops."

But she insists she remains the same writer.

"I don't think writing in English has changed me," she said. "There isn't a different vision of the world. The message is the same."

At the very least, however, language interferes. Ms. Ferré, who translated two of her Spanish books into English, one of them with a collaborator—"Sweet Diamond Dust," a novella and three stories, and "The Youngest Doll," a short-story collection—has now translated her two English novels into Spanish herself. She regards them as "Spanish versions" rather than literal translations because she adds and takes out details, changes metaphors and tinkers with her characters.

Quintín Mendizabal, for example, the patriarch in "The House on the Lagoon," is "less unpleasant, nicer and more human" in English, she said, whereas in Spanish, he is "a scoundrel who is not worthy of forgiveness." Ms. Ferré cannot quite explain why, except that Spanish and English resonate differently. Spanish-speaking "Quintín" may reflect machismo in Puerto Rican society, she said.

Similarly, her mother's long-held belief that Americans make better husbands than Puerto Ricans may have subconsciously crept into the shaping of the character, she said with a smile. (Thrice married—two husbands were Puerto Rican, one Mexican—Ms. Ferré said she had no way of knowing whether her mother was right.)

Ms. Ferré, whose father, Luis A. Ferré, is a former Governor of Puerto Rico, comes from a wealthy family not unlike the aristocratic sugar-plantation owners and cement tycoons she writes about, although she stresses that her novels are strictly fiction. Her brother publishes Puerto Rico's largest daily newspaper, El Nuevo Día.

Although her family name is synonymous with the island's statehood movement—her father founded the pro-statehood New Progressive Party—Ms. Ferré, like many other Puerto Rican writers and artists, embraced independence ideals and even voted for the Puerto Rico Independence Party candidate who ran against her father in the 1972 governor's election. But last March, she surprised and angered many of her admirers when she wrote in an Op-Ed article in [t]he *New York Times* that she no longer favored independence and would vote for statehood instead in the referendum scheduled for December.

She wrote that independence had once been "the only honorable solution," because under statehood, "losing our language and culture would have been a form of spiritual suicide." Language is a crucial issue in the political debate over whether Puerto Rico should choose statehood or independence.

"But conditions have changed," she argued in the article, noting that Hispanic people are the fastest growing minority in the United States. "Bilingualism and multiculturalism are vital aspects of American society."

Her change of heart caused a bit of an uproar here. In a sarcastic reply that appeared in her brother's newspaper, Ana Lydia Vega, another Puerto Rican writer, dubbed Ms. Ferré's arguments "a sad apology for assimilation." Ms. Vega wrote that she was not as indignant as she was disillusioned.

Ms. Ferré responded with silence. She said she abhorred political intransigence, adding that she did not want to get into a public dispute. Still, she maintains that Puerto Rico's cultural integrity need not be jeopardized as long as the United States accepts Puerto Rico as it is.

"People are proud of who they are," she said. "Why should they be maimed?"

As a bilingual writer, Ms. Ferré, who also speaks French, sees nothing but advantages to her command of languages. When she tours the United States, she said, Hispanic readers thank her for writing in English because they say they have long forgotten their Spanish.

She admonishes them to hold on to their native tongue. English, she said, has made her grow as a writer but could never be a substitute for Spanish.

"Language," Ms. Ferré said, "is like your skin."

Mireya Navarro's article is fascinating because it demonstrates not only the power of language to shape our identities and personalities, but also some unexpected benefits of learning another language.

Now that we have a little better picture of what language means in our lives, we can proceed directly to the current debate over bilingual education in America's schools. First, we need some background information, and we begin by considering the scope of the problem. About 2.8 million American elementary and secondary students are limited-English proficient (LEP). Although three-quarters of these students speak Spanish, the rest speak one of more than 180 foreign languages, and all need assistance to learn normal school subjects. In the 1990s we have seen the number of American LEP students double, and many more are expected in the next decade. Half the nation's school districts have undertaken some sort of program to assist LEP students, but a severe shortage of LEP certified teachers makes the task difficult. As a result of this shortage, a third of LEP students receive assistance neither in speaking English nor in understanding their regular school subjects.

Bilingual education (BE), which is using two languages in the classroom, is found in many nations around the world, and has been employed in some American schools since this nation's founding. Typical BE classes include instruction in both languages and regular subjects such as math and social science, in both English and the second language. Although it takes an average LEP student only two years to learn basic conversational English, at least seven years are normally required to learn English sufficiently to succeed in secondary and higher education. BE proponents claim that many BE programs have successfully helped students become academically competent in both English and a foreign language, providing them with valuable social and employment skills. A study conducted at George Mason University found that graduates of good BE programs surpass students whose native language is English in regular academic subjects. The Bilingual Education Act of 1968 provided funds for BE programs which, in 1994, amounted to $176 million. These voluntary federal assistance programs train 4,000 BE teachers annually, but most BE programs are funded primarily with state and local funds. BE advocates point to the Calexico and Healdsburg school districts in California as examples of areas in which BE has helped lower the school dropout and raise the college attendance rates.

The primary opposition to BE comes in the form of the "English Only" (EO) movement. Notable EO proponent (1996 Republican presidential nominee) Robert Dole maintains that "Alternative language education should stop and English should be acknowledged once and for all as the official language of the United States." Dole believes that "Schools should provide the language classes our immigrants and their families need, as long as their purpose is the teaching of English.... But we must stop the practice of multilingual education as a means of instilling ethnic pride or as therapy for low self-esteem or out of elitist guilt over a culture built on the traditions of the West." Dole's sentiments are praised by two national organizations, English First and U.S. English, which have succeeded in getting EO legislation passed in 23 states. This legislation prohibits state schools from offering bilingual instruction. Although an English Language Amendment to the U.S. Constitution was first offered to Congress in 1981, it has yet to pass. The following *New York Times* articles (on pages 101–113) provide considerable information about arguments made by both sides in this controversy. As you read them, try to identify what you think are the real issues in the controversy, as opposed to issues used merely for argument or publicity.

The New York Times

October 14, 1998

Bilingual for Its Own Sake,
an Alternative School Bucks the Tide

By Vivian S. Toy

Michelle Leung's kindergarten classroom at Public School 184 on the Lower East Side looks much like any other, with a few hard-to-miss exceptions.

The tags taped onto her students' pint-size tables have their names written in bold block letters and also in painterly Chinese characters. Objects throughout the room—the door, the clock, the closet—also bear signs identifying them in English and Chinese. Indeed, the entire school day is infused with both languages because P.S. 184, which opened last month with two kindergarten classes, is the first public school in the nation designed to teach fluency in English and Mandarin Chinese.

The school, one of more than 150 small, alternative public schools that have opened across the city in the last few years, is also known as the Shuang Wen Academy, after the Chinese for "double language." But it is a distinct departure from the traditional bilingual programs that are criticized in many parts of the country these days as hindrances to immigrants' learning the language of their new land.

Traditional bilingual programs seek to educate non-English-speaking children by teaching them in their native language until they are confident enough to learn exclusively in English. These classes, which remain widely accepted in New York, generally teach nonlinguistic subjects like science, history or math.

Shuang Wen, where most of the students speak at least some English, has another, almost opposite goal. Like a small number of other dual-language schools across the country, it seeks to teach students the language and culture of their homeland for their own sake.

"We're different from a traditional bilingual program where children are taught in their mother tongue just long enough to get them fluent in English," said Ling-Ling Chou, the head of the school. "Here we teach in both languages, and we want them to master both languages."

For the parents, nearly all of them immigrants or children of immigrants, it is a way to help the children weave together their Chinese and American selves.

As such, it serves much the same purpose as the dozens of weekend Chinese schools across the city, where children study Chinese language and culture.

"When I grew up I saw a lot of kids who rebelled against being Chinese and who rejected what they were," said Larry Lee, a social worker and one of the leaders of the group of parents and community activists who led the campaign to create Shuang Wen. "With this school, my hope is that these kids can be comfortable with who they are and also be comfortable being American."

Even so, Shuang Wen met a certain amount of opposition in the planning stages, when some non-Chinese teachers and residents of the district said the school would be a barrier to assimilation.

At the moment, all 40 of the children at Shuang Wen are of Chinese descent, though fewer than a quarter speak Mandarin, the main language of China and Taiwan. Many are fluent in Cantonese, which is still the predominant dialect in Chinatown, and a few speak no Chinese at all.

But school officials hope that as the school grows, grade by grade, it will attract a more diverse student body—one that includes children of other ethnic groups.

The bulk of the regular school day, until 3 P.M., is taught in English and runs like a typical kindergarten class. They work on the alphabet. They read from picture books. They paste leaves onto construction paper. They nap. They have lunch.

Ms. Leung uses Chinese sparingly, when a student doesn't understand an instruction she has given in English. The teacher of the other class, Aline Jaquez, doesn't speak any Chinese and so relies on hand gestures and actions to communicate with her native Chinese speakers. She also relies heavily on two full-time volunteers who speak Mandarin and who sometimes help break up the school day with short Chinese programs like a puppet show or an art project.

The core Chinese instruction, however, comes from 3 until 5:30, from teachers paid with private funds raised mainly from foundations.

To combat the fatigue that the children naturally feel after a full school day, the Chinese teachers emphasize music and movement.

One day recently, a teacher, Julie Wei, got the children up on their feet, punched on the tape player and used grand, exaggerated gestures to lead them through a song describing a child's morning regimen. Even the children who spoke no Chinese followed along eagerly as they mimed and sang about washing their faces, brushing their teeth, strapping on their book bags and waving goodbye to Mom and Dad.

The children have been strategically grouped at tables with at least one student fluent in Mandarin and one fluent in English. "They learn a lot from each other because at this age, they like to imitate one another," Ms. Wei said. "The best part is that they don't even realize that they're teaching each other."

Lee, a third-generation Chinese-American who says he often regrets his own inability to speak Chinese, said he and a group of Asian-American educators had talked about starting a school like Shuang Wen for nearly 10 years. But it wasn't until 1996 that they formally proposed it and won a grant from New Visions for Public Schools, a foundation that has helped establish more than 30 alternative public schools since 1992.

When designing the school day, Shuang Wen's planning committee had a fairly limited number of models. San Francisco has three schools that teach Cantonese, and there are fewer than 200 Spanish dual-language schools across the country, many of which are patterned after Canadian schools that teach in French and English.

Maria Carlo, a professor at the Harvard Graduate School of Education, said the hardest job of any dual-language school is finding a way to educate everyone while still meeting the different language needs of each child. "A very delicate balance needs to be achieved there in order to make it work," she said.

Paula Grande marvels at how much Chinese her 5-year-old daughter, You Jing Streeter, has picked up in just a few short weeks. You Jing is one of two children at the school who were adopted from China by American parents; in the three years since Ms. Grande and her husband adopted You Jing, they have made a concerted effort to bring Chinese culture into their family life.

Ms. Grande said You Jing was clearly a little frustrated after the first day of school because she spoke no Mandarin. But she said You Jing now comes home each day repeating Chinese phrases and singing songs.

"We took her out of her culture, but we don't want her to lose it," Ms. Grande said. "And Shuang Wen, we think, will help her be more comfortable in the culture she was born in."

The New York Times

June 5, 1998

The Reply, It Turned Out, Was Bilingual: No

BY DON TERRY

LOS ANGELES—English can still be a riddle to 60-year-old Rosario Gomez, even after three decades here in a house with red and yellow roses in the front yard on Chicago Street.

But her two adult children, both of whom were born in Los Angeles and enrolled in bilingual education classes in grade school, have good jobs, bright futures and are literate and fluent in English and Spanish.

That, Mrs. Gomez explained, is why her family voted "no" in Tuesday's primary election here on Proposition 227, the nationally watched initiative that will dismantle 30 years of bilingual education in California. The measure easily passed with 61 percent of the vote. But despite pre-election polls suggesting it would also carry a majority of Hispanic voters, fewer than 4 in 10 Hispanic Californians who voted favored the proposition in the end, after a blitz against the measure by almost every elected Hispanic official in the state.

Still, in more than two dozen interviews on the largely Hispanic east side of Los Angeles, even some of those who voted "no," like Mrs. Gomez's daughter, Elva Osorio, expressed deep concern about the state of bilingual education.

"When I was in school, bilingual education was much better than it is now," Mrs. Osorio said. "I voted 'no,' but I knew it was going to lose, because a lot of people are upset that their kids don't know how to speak English and they're in the fifth grade." Getting Hispanic Californians like the Gomez family to vote "yes" was a priority for Ron Unz, a conservative

Republican and the main sponsor and financial backer of the measure, which will essentially eliminate bilingual education in the state if it survives court challenges. His campaign spent a lot of time and energy wooing Hispanic voters, hoping to avoid the racially charged atmosphere that surrounded earlier ballot initiative drives in California, on subjects like affirmative action.

Yet, despite those efforts, words like "racism," "prejudice" and "discrimination" often came up in interviews after Tuesday's balloting.

"I believe it is racism towards us," said Rito Mateos, a 32-year-old gardener, who voted "no." "This is a threat to the community. It's not going to stop here." Mrs. Gomez said she knew of no one on her block who had voted [who] supported the measure. "I think it passed because a lot of American people are tired of us," she said.

No matter how they voted, the Hispanic parents, telephone operators, construction workers and others interviewed agreed on one issue: for immigrant children, whether they are from Mexico or Vietnam, the key to unlocking the treasures of the United States is to learn English as quickly as possible.

"I voted 'no,' but it was hard for me to make up my mind," said Gloria Luna, 65, whose great-grandmother was "born in this state when it was Mexico." Mrs. Luna said she decided to vote against the measure because so many educators opposed it, saying its provision to provide non-English speaking-public school children with only one year of intensive language training before sending them into mainstream classes would do more harm than good.

"It is so important for Hispanics to learn English," Mrs. Luna said, "but one year is much too fast." Like Mrs. Gomez and Mr. Mateos, Mrs. Luna said she suspected that prejudice, not pedagogy, was at the root of the campaign to eliminate bilingual education.

"I think a lot of people who voted don't know anything about education," Mrs. Luna said.

Steve Feria, 44, agreed with Mrs. Luna, up to a point. A flight instructor, M[r]. Feria was working in his family's wallet stand on Olvera Street when he took time to talk about the initiative. He said anyone with the slightest knowledge of education would have supported Proposition 227—as he did.

"I honestly believe, the only way to learn English is to be immersed in it," said Mr. Feria, who did not take part in bilingual classes when he was in school. "I wouldn't have a job as a flight instructor if I didn't have the proper English skills." Mr. Feria said the teachers and politicians who opposed the measure did so because they were afraid they would lose their money and influence if bilingual education was eliminated.

"It's all a money grab," Mr. Feria said. "We do our kids a disfavor by putting them in bilingual education." As she walked through Olvera Street near downtown, Mirian Luis, 22, a paralegal's assistant, said she voted "no" because her nieces and nephews were doing well in bilingual education programs.

"It's a joke," Ms. Luis said of the proposition. "I mean, how are the kids going to learn?" A few miles away, on Cesar E. Chavez Avenue, George Ramos was hanging orange and yellow fliers, balloons and a Mexican flag advertising his travel business. He voted "yes" on Proposition 226, because, he said, "This is America." "Everyone is supposed to speak English," Mr. Ramos said. "If you go to France, you don't ask for bilingual education. If you go to China, you cannot request bilingual education. They will kick you out of there." At El Mercado, a warehouse-like complex of shops and restaurants not far from Chavez Avenue, Manuel Romero, a retired General Motors worker, said he voted for the proposition because there were not enough qualified teachers to staff bilingual education programs adequately.

In fact, the state Department of Education said it was 20,000 bilingual education teachers short of what it needed. The state said there were 1.4 million public school pupils with limited English skills in California. Thirty percent of those students are in bilingual classes.

"If we had quality teachers," Mr. Romero said, "it would be O.K."

Jerry and Diana Ontiveros voted "no." They grew up in a largely white neighborhood in Whittier and attended Roman Catholic schools before going to college and getting married. They did not take part in bilingual programs. They were surrounded by English speakers everywhere they went, which is not the case for many immigrant children who often live in segregated and isolated neighborhoods.

"I've been assimilated into the mainstream culture all of my life," Mr. Ontiveros said. "Others haven't had the opportunities I've had and that's why I support bilingual education." Ramon Moreno, a 30-year-old teacher's assistant, said he voted for the proposition.

"I felt like maybe bilingual education is like a handicap or something," Mr. Moreno said. "It gives the kids too much leeway not to learn." Maria Tovar said she voted for Proposition 227, but by mistake.

Ms. Tovar said she supported bilingual education and thought that a "yes" vote meant saving it.

When she came to the United States 25 years ago at the age of 14, Ms. Tovar said, she did not speak or understand English and struggled in school to learn without a bilingual program. Several of her classmates were not as determined, she said, and they dropped out, never learning the language.

"It was very, very tough," she said, "trying to learn English without bilingual education."

The New York Times

October 3, 1998

California Still Debates
Bilingual Education

By Don Terry

LOS ANGELES—Bilingual education in California was supposed to be in a grave by now, essentially killed when residents voted last spring to end it.

The ballot initiative, supported by 61 percent of the voters, sought to replace 30 years of using Spanish and other foreign languages to help immigrant children in the state learn to read, write and speak English with a method that uses "nearly all" English instruction.

But more than a month into the current school term, bilingual education is clearly still breathing. The reasons are a subject of hot debate.

Supporters of the initiative, Proposition 227, assert that school districts and the education bureaucracy are resisting the will of the voters, taking advantage of loopholes to preserve a rejected method of teaching.

Critics of the proposition see the bumpy transition as a result of confusion, reluctance on the part of some parents and teachers to push children into instruction they are not ready for, and even basic logistical issues like the lack of textbooks.

What is clear is that the fight over Proposition 227 is not over yet.

Doug Stone, a spokesman for the state Education Department, said he had heard of no open defiance of the law and "when push came to shove, virtually all of the districts are complying."

Some do not agree with that assessment.

"A lot of people are trying to loosely interpret and undermine this law," said Sean Walsh, a spokesman for Gov. Pete Wilson, a Republican and a critic of bilingual education. "The law says 'nearly all' should be taught in English. But many districts are using 40 percent Spanish and 60 percent English."

The law does not define what "nearly all" means, so there is much disagreement over what constitutes compliance.

Elena Soto-Chapa, the statewide education director for the Mexican American Legal Defense and Educational Fund, which has gone to court seeking to block the initiative, said that how the hundreds of school districts across the state defined "nearly all" was "just all over the spectrum."

Ms. Soto-Chapa said some districts were using a 60–40 English to foreign language formula while others were using 70–30 or 80–20. "There's a lot of confusion," she said. "It's a very political, murky environment right now."

The Los Angeles United School District, with 681,505 students the second largest in the country behind New York City, offers two programs for pupils with limited English ability: Model A and Model B. In Model A, the classes are taught virtually all in English. In Model B, 65 percent to 70 percent of the classes are taught in English.

Alice Callaghan, one of the leading proponents of Proposition 227, said "L.A. is absolutely out of compliance."

The state Education Department has set up a study group to help districts implement the law.

"We realized that before June 2 and after June 2 there would be more questions than answers," Stone said, referring to the day the initiative was approved. "But that isn't a sign from heaven that school districts can thwart the law."

Out of the 5.5 million public school pupils in California, about 1.4 million have a limited understanding of English, but only 30 percent of them were enrolled in bilingual education programs last year. The rest were in classes in which teachers used nearly all English. There were not enough qualified teachers for bilingual classes.

Under Proposition 227, some parents are eligible to request that their children be retained in a bilingual program, and such waivers can be granted by a school district under three circumstances: The child has a physical or psychological need to be in bilingual education, the child is over 10 years old or the child speaks English.

But the question of waivers is also the subject of intense and varied interpretation and debate. Before a waiver can be granted, a child must spend the first 30 days of school in a class taught primarily in English. That period has now expired for about 25,000 Los Angeles pupils with limited English skills who started the new year in late summer. Although many expected a wave of request for waivers, only about 1,300 have been sought so far, said Forrest Ross, director of language acquisition for the Los Angeles district.

Ms. Soto-Chapa said, "I think a lot of parents are taking a wait and see approach."

At the Logan Street School in Los Angeles, a few blocks from Dodger Stadium, parents of 250 of the 360 pupils eligible have asked for and received waivers. Those children are now in bilingual classes.

"We're not trying to circumvent the law," said Logan Street's principal, May Arakaki. "We're just giving the parents the options they and their children deserve and are entitled to."

Mrs. Arakaki and her staff have had to do some fancy juggling. Mrs. Arakaki had to move three children whose parents signed waivers into Helen Trevino's second-grade class, which is primarily bilingual, and move three others into an English-immersion class.

Still, Ms. Trevino has a class of nine bilingual pupils and six who are taught primarily in English, forcing her to go from table to table and tongue to tongue. Ideally, the class would be either all bilingual or virtually all English.

"I'm for bilingual education," Ms. Trevino said. "But the new law has passed and we have to deal with it."

In one twist, 39 of the nearly 1,000 schools districts in California—including Los Angeles, San Diego, Fresno and Oakland—have requested waivers of some kind to teaching all classes primarily in English—whether for individual schools or for entire districts.

But in August, the state Board of Education, whose 11 members are appointed by the governor, refused to consider the waiver requests, saying it did not have the authority to grant them to districts.

"The initiative was very clear about waivers," said Bill Lucia, executive director of the state school board. "And it doesn't say anything about districtwide waivers."

After the board refused to hear the requests, the districts of Oakland, Hayward and Berkeley took the board to court, demanding that it be forced to do so.

"We feel that bilingual education works and we feel that our community believes in bilingual education," said Sue Piper, a spokeswoman for the 53,000-pupil Oakland Unified School District. "That's not to say it's perfect. But our test scores show that the children who graduate from bilingual education do very well."

Alameda County Superior Court Judge Henry Needham ruled last month that the board had to hear the districts' wai[v]er requests. The board appealed the decision and voted to postpone action on the requests pending the outcome of the appeal. That could be months, and in the meantime the districts are required to implement the proposition.

Wilson had urged the board to appeal Needham's decision, saying his decision "could potentially eviscerate Proposition 227."

Lucia said that some of the board members were also concerned that they might be sued by proponents of the proposition if they ruled on the waivers before the issue of the board's authority had been determined in the appeal.

"It could require individual board members to get lawyers," he said. "It's a serious matter. It's a question of losing your house."

The initiative says that teachers and administrators who implement the law improperly can be held liable.

"We're going to be suing soon," said Ms. Callaghan, a leading supporter of the proposition. "We won't let this go on much longer."

The threat of lawsuits has also had a chilling effect on teachers. Hundreds of teachers in Los Angeles signed a petition last spring pledging open rebellion if Proposition 227 passed. The teachers vowed to risk being sued and dismissed by continuing to use bilingual education methods in their classrooms. But so far, the rebellion has not materialized—at least not openly.

"Open defiance would be dismissal, and that was made very clear to us," said Steve Zimmer a member of On Campus, the teachers' group that organized the pledge of resistance. "But you certainly still have defiance. It's just being done behind closed doors."

Zimmer said that some teachers were simply teaching how they had always taught immigrant children, using bilingual methods, while others who otherwise comply with the law were still using a lot of bilingual methods because they did not yet have the books and other materials necessary to put the proposition into effect.

"There aren't enough books," he said. "There are stories about fourth graders using kindergarten books."

Still, Zimmer said, the majority of teachers are doing their best to comply with the law.

"Even though we did the pledge," he said, "I can't in good conscience tell a teacher to let this fail so we can get rid of it. The efforts of teachers not to damage children is what is making this work at all."

But Ms. Callaghan said she received almost daily reports of widespread non-compliance by teachers and districts.

"Name me a district that is not defying the law," she said. "There will be less Spanish spoken, but that doesn't mean they will teach English immersion. The law required that bilingual education be replaced, not mended. It's going to be a very unfortunate year."

Yet at individual schools like Logan Street in Los Angeles, it is more a year of improvisation, of trying to accommodate and educate at the same time.

Gloria Rodriguez has two children at Logan, a daughter, Christina, 8, a third grader, and a son, Gabriel, 9, a fourth grader. Her daughter began school in bilingual classes but tested high enough to move into classes taught in English before Proposition 227 became the law.

Mrs. Rodriguez signed a waiver for her son.

"He's not ready yet," she said. "My daughter is doing very well, and I think it is because of bilingual education. When she goes to college, she wants to learn Japanese and French. That will be four languages she will know how to speak and write. Employers will love her."

Questions for Class Discussion or Debate

As you read the *New York Times* articles and conduct further research, many questions may come to your mind. If you plan to debate bilingual education issues in class, you may want to consider arguing positions related to the following statements:

- Americans should work toward a common culture.
- Language is central to human identity.
- Bilingual education encourages disunity.
- Facility with more than one language is beneficial to all students.
- English-only laws promote racism.

Resources for Class Debates and Further Study

Bilingual Education and English Only on the Internet

The following are three prominent pro-bilingual education organizations:

The National Association for Bilingual Education
www.nabe.org
National Council of La Raza
www.nclr.org
The National Clearinghouse for Bilingual Education (NCBE)
www.ncbe.gwu.edu

The following are three prominent English-Only organizations:

English First
www.englishfirst.org
U.S. English
www.us-english.org
English Language Advocates
www.elausa.org

Further Reference

Baker, Colin, ed. *Encyclopedia of Bilingualism and Bilingual Education.* Multilingual Matters. 1998.

Bangura, Abdul Karim, and Martin C. Muo. *United States Congress and Bilingual Education.* Peter Lang Publishing. 1998.

Bartolome, Lilia I., Joe L. Kincheloe, and Shirley Strinberg, eds. *The Misteaching of Academic Discourses—The Politics of Language in the Classroom.* Westview Press. 1998.

Cenoz, Jasone, and Fred Genesee, eds. *Beyond Bilingualism: Multilingualism and Multilingual Education*. Multilingual Matters. 1998.

Darder, Antonia, Rodolfo D. Torres, Henry Gutierrez, and Andoria Darde, eds. *Latinos and Education: A Critical Reader*. Routledge. 1997.

Durguno glu, Aydin Y., and Ludo th Verhoeven, eds. *Literacy Development in a Multilingual Context: Cross-Cultural Perspectives*. Lawrence Erlbaum Assoc. 1998.

Faltis, Christian, and Paula Wolfe, eds. *So Much to Say—Adolescents, Bilingualism, and ESL in the Secondary School*. Teachers College Press. 1998.

Kloss, Heinz. *The American Bilingual Tradition*. Center for Applied Linguistics. 1998.

Krashen, Stephen D. *Under Attack—The Case against Bilingual Education*. Language Education Associates. 1997.

Porter, Rosalie Pedaling. *Forked Tongue: The Politics of Bilingual Education*. Transaction Publications. 1996.